# 10
## MINUTE GUIDE TO

# WINDOWS 95

by Trudi Reisner

*A Division of Macmillan Computer Publishing*
*201 West 103rd St., Indianapolis, Indiana 46290 USA*

*To Bob Jones. Thank you for making me laugh.*

*Many thanks to the people at Que who have helped me with this project. First, thanks to Martha O'Sullivan for signing me to write this. Thanks to Heather Stith for her help on developing this book. Thanks to Mark Enochs and Julie McNamee for keeping the manuscript in great shape. And thanks to all the other people I worked with at Que who helped turn this book around on such an aggressive schedule.*

## ©1995 Que Corporation

International Standard Book Number: 1-56761-515-5

Library of Congress Catalog Card Number: 94-72081

97 96 95    8 7 6 5 4 3 2 1

Interpretation of the printing code: the rightmost number of the first series of numbers is the year of the book's printing; the rightmost number of the second series of numbers is the number of the book's printing. For example, a printing code of 95-1 shows that the first printing of the book occurred in 1995.

*Printed in the United States of America*

**Publisher** *Roland Elgey*
**Vice-President and Publisher** *Marie Butler-Knight*
**Editorial Services Director** *Elizabeth Keaffaber*
**Publishing Manager** *Barry Pruett*
**Managing Editor** *Michael Cunningham*
**Development Editors** *Heather Stith, Seta Frantz*
**Production Editors** *Mark Enochs, Julie McNamee*
**Copy Editors** *Audra Gable, Silvette Pope*
**Technical Specialist** *Cari Skaggs*
**Cover Designer** *Dan Armstrong*
**Designer** *Barb Kordesh*
**Indexer** *Mary Jane Frisby*
**Production Team** *Claudia Bell, DiMonique Ford, George Hanlin, Damon Jordan, Daryl Kessler, Beth Lewis, Kaylene Riemen, Clair Schweinler, Brenda Sims, Tim Taylor, Michael Thomas, Paul Wilson, Karen Gregor-York*

*Special thanks to Martin Wyatt for ensuring the technical accuracy of this book.*

# CONTENTS

# INTRODUCTION

"There aren't enough hours in the day." It's a common complaint. Time is a commodity everyone can use more of. When it comes to working with your computer, Windows 95 can save you time. How? Windows makes the computer easier to use and increases the "fun factor."

## THE WHAT AND WHY OF WINDOWS 95

Windows 95 is a graphical user interface (GUI). This GUI comes with useful applications, including a word processor (WordPad) and a drawing program (Paint).

 **Graphical User Interface** A GUI (pronounced "gooey") makes interacting with your computer easy. You usually use a mouse to point at and select icons (small pictures that most often represent files or application programs), and you choose operations (commands from menus) to perform on those icons. A GUI is an alternative to a *command-line interface*, where text commands are entered from the keyboard.

Why use Windows 95? Windows 95 makes using your computer faster and easier in the following ways:

- You can work in more than one application at a time. By clicking a button on the taskbar, you can switch between applications without having to close one to open another. You can also copy information from one application to the other.

- The graphical user interface is easy to figure out and remember, so you'll be up and running quickly. Once you get started, you'll be surprised how quickly your "educated guesses" become correct ones.

- All application programs designed for Windows 95 use similar keyboard and mouse operations to select objects and choose commands. To a great extent, once you've learned one application, you've learned part of them all.

- Video and graphics applications run smoothly so that multimedia applications, games, and graphics programs, such as CorelDRAW, really shine.

Windows 95's GUI provides a common approach to using a variety of applications for your computer. With just a little effort, Windows 95 is fast, easy, and fun to learn.

## WHY THE 10 MINUTE GUIDE TO WINDOWS 95?

The *10 Minute Guide to Windows 95* can save even more of your precious time. Each lesson is designed to be completed in 10 minutes or less, so you'll be up to snuff in basic Windows skills quickly.

Though you can jump between lessons, starting at the beginning is a good plan. The bare-bones basics are covered first; more advanced topics are covered later. Whatever you do, don't miss the inside front and back covers. The inside front cover of this book features instructions for installing Windows on your system. The inside back cover contains a typical Windows 95 window with its elements.

## CONVENTIONS USED IN THIS BOOK

To help you move through the lessons easily, these conventions are used:

| | |
|---|---|
| On-screen text | On-screen text appears in **bold** type. |
| What you type | Information you type appears in **bold color** type. |
| Items you select | Commands, options, and icons you select or keys you press appear in color type. |

In telling you to choose menu commands, this book uses the format *menu title, menu command*. For example, the statement "choose File, Properties" means to "open the File menu and select the Properties command."

In addition to these conventions, the *10 Minute Guide to Windows 95* uses the following icons to identify helpful information:

**Plain English**   New or unfamiliar terms are defined in (you got it) "plain English."

**Timesaver Tips**   Look here for ideas that cut corners and confusion.

**Upgrade Tips**   These tips explain how a Windows 95 procedure is different from or similar to a Windows 3.1 procedure.

**Panic Button**   This icon identifies areas where new users often run into trouble, and offers practical solutions to those problems.

## TRADEMARKS

All terms mentioned in this book that are known to be trademarks have been appropriately capitalized. Que cannot attest to the accuracy of this information. Use of a term in this book should not be regarded as affecting the validity of any trademark or service mark.

# NAVIGATING THE WINDOWS 95 DESKTOP

*In this lesson, you'll learn about the parts of the Windows 95 desktop and how to use a mouse to manipulate items on the desktop.*

## UNDERSTANDING THE WINDOWS 95 DESKTOP

Once Windows 95 is installed on your system (see the inside front cover of this book for instructions on how to do this), you go directly to the Windows 95 desktop each time you start your computer. As you can see in Figure 1.1, the Windows 95 desktop is made up of several components. These components are used throughout Windows 95 and Windows applications to make it easy for you to get your work done. You can customize the desktop by adding more components so that Windows 95 works the way that you do (see Lesson 20).

The components of the desktop include:

**Icons**  Icons are pictures that represent programs (Microsoft Excel, WordPerfect, and so on), files (documents, spreadsheets, graphics), printer information (setup options, installed fonts), and computer information (hard and floppy disk drives). Although when you first see the Windows 95 desktop, you only have two icons (My Computer and the Recycle Bin), icons are used throughout Windows 95 and Windows applications. Icons come in two sizes, large and small, and Windows 95 uses four types of icons: program, file, printer, and computer. I will point out each type of icon as it is introduced in the book.

**Desktop**   This is the area that takes up the entire background of the screen.

**Mouse pointer**   The on-screen pointer (usually an arrow) that you use to select items and choose commands. You move the pointer by moving the mouse across your desk or mouse pad. You'll learn how to use the mouse later in this lesson.

**My Computer**   The My Computer icon gives you access to a window in which you can browse through the contents of your computer or find out information about the disk drives, control panel, and printers that you have on your computer.

**Recycle Bin**   The Recycle Bin serves as your electronic trash can. You drag unwanted files, folders, or other icons to the Recycle Bin, and the Recycle Bin appears to have papers spilling over the top of it. To permanently delete the items, first double-click on the Recycle Bin icon to open its window. Select the items you want to delete, pull down the File menu and choose Empty Recycle Bin. Windows asks you for your confirmation.

**Start button**   You click the Start button to display the Start menu, which contains a list of commands that enable you to get to work quickly and easily. The Start menu contains commands for launching programs, opening the most recently used files, changing settings, finding files or folders, accessing Help topics, running a program by entering a specific command line, and shutting down Windows 95.

**Taskbar**   Click a button on the taskbar to either launch a program or switch to a different task. For each application that you open, a button appears on the taskbar. When you use more than one application at a time, you can see the names of all the open applications on the taskbar. At any time, you can click the appropriate button on the taskbar to work with an open application.

Initially, the taskbar appears at the bottom of the screen. However, you can move it to the top, left, or right side of the screen to suit your needs. For example, if you were using the Microsoft Word for Windows program and the taskbar appeared above the status bar, you might want to drag the taskbar to the top of the screen and position it below the toolbars, where it is more convenient for use.

A clock at the right end of the taskbar displays the current time, and if you have a sound card, the Volume Control icon appears next to the clock. The Volume Control feature enables you to control the volume for sounds played through your computer speaker and multimedia devices.

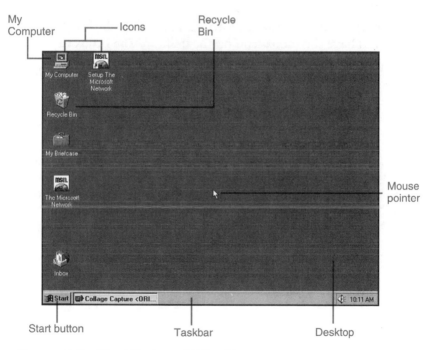

**FIGURE 1.1** The Windows 95 Desktop.

**Taskbar/Task List**   Windows 95's taskbar is different from the Windows 3.1 task list because the taskbar is accessible at all times. In Windows 3.1, you had to press Ctrl+Esc to access the Task List and press Alt+Tab to switch to a different task.

**Network Neighborhood**   If your computer is on a network, you have another icon on the desktop called Network Neighborhood. Double-click the Network Neighborhood icon to browse through your network and see what it contains. This icon also provides information on mapped drives and interfaces.

**Inbox**   If you installed Microsoft Exchange during setup, you have the Inbox icon on the desktop. The Inbox functions as a central place to get information from various information services, such as CompuServe, electronic mail systems, and Microsoft Fax software. Double-click the Inbox icon to send and receive mail and faxes on your network.

**My Briefcase**   If you chose the Portable or Custom option to install Briefcase, you have the My Briefcase icon on your desktop. You can use Briefcase to keep copies of your files updated at home on your main computer or on the road on your portable computer.

# USING THE MOUSE

You can use the mouse to quickly select an icon or window, among other things. The process involves two steps: pointing and clicking.

To *point* to an object (icon, window title bar, and so on), move the mouse across your desk or mouse pad until the on-screen mouse pointer touches the object. You may have to pick up the mouse and reposition it if you run out of room on your desk.

To *click*, point the mouse pointer at the object you want to select, and then quickly press and release the left mouse button. If the object is an icon or window, it becomes highlighted.

When you're pointing at an object, you can also click the right mouse button (*right-click*) on it to select it. Simply press and release the right mouse button once. If the object is an icon, it becomes highlighted. If you right-click on the desktop, the taskbar, or a taskbar button, a menu opens. You can perform many shortcuts in Windows 95 by right-clicking. These shortcuts are mentioned throughout the book.

When you *double-click* on an item, you point to the item and press and release the left mouse button twice in rapid succession. Double-clicking is often the easiest way to perform a task; for example, you can open a window by double-clicking its icon.

You can also use the mouse to move an object (usually a window, dialog box, or icon) to a new position on-screen. You do this by dragging the object. To *drag* an object to a new location on-screen, point to the object, press and hold the left mouse button, move the mouse to a new location, and release the mouse button. The object moves with the mouse cursor.

In this lesson, you learned about the parts of the Windows 95 desktop and how to use the mouse to manipulate items on the desktop. In the next lesson, you'll learn how to work with windows.

# WORKING WITH A WINDOW

*In this lesson, you will learn how to open a window, use scroll bars, resize a window, move a window, and close a window.*

## WHAT IS A WINDOW?

A *window* is a rectangular area of the screen in which you view program folders, files, or icons. The window is made up of several components (see Figure 2.1) that are the same for all windows in Windows 95 and Windows applications and make it easy for you to manage your work.

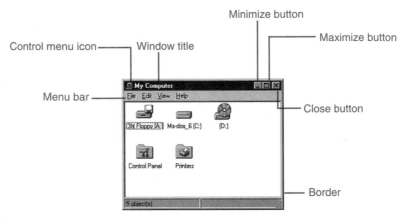

FIGURE 2.1   The My Computer window.

**Newly Styled Components**   For the most part, the components in the Windows 95 and Windows 3.1 windows are the same. The main difference is that the title bar, the Minimize, Maximize, and Restore buttons, and the Control menu have new looks in Windows 95. In addition, Windows 3.1 windows don't have Close buttons, and the Minimize command varies slightly in that it reduces the window to a button on the taskbar, while in Windows 3.1 it reduces the window to an icon on the desktop.

# OPENING WINDOWS

To open a window from an icon, double-click the icon. For example, point at the My Computer icon and double-click. If you do it correctly, the My Computer icon opens up to the My Computer window.

You can also use a shortcut menu to open a window. Just point to the icon and click the right mouse button, and a shortcut menu appears. Select Open on the shortcut menu, and the icon opens into a window.

# USING SCROLL BARS

*Scroll bars* appear along the bottom and right edges of a window when text, graphics, or icons in a window take up more space than the area shown. Using scroll bars, you can move up, down, left, or right in a window.

Figure 2.2 shows an example. Because the Control Panel's contents are not fully visible in the window, scroll bars are present on the bottom and right sides of the window. The following steps show you one way to use the scroll bars to view items outside the window:

1. To see an object that is down and to the right of the viewable area of the window, point at the down arrow located on the bottom of the vertical scroll bar.

2. Click on the arrow, and the window's contents scroll up.

3. Click on the scroll arrow on the right side of the horizontal scroll bar, and the window's contents move left.

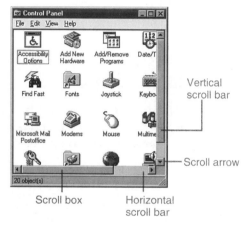

**Figure 2.2**    Scroll bars.

By its size within the scroll bar, the scroll box depicts how much of a window is not visible. If you know approximately where something is in a window (maybe two-thirds of the way down, for example), you might want to drag the scroll box. To drag a scroll box and move quickly to a distant area of the window (top or bottom, left or right), use this technique:

1. Point to the scroll box in the scroll bar and hold down the left mouse button.

2. Drag the scroll box to the new location.

3. Release the mouse button.

Sometimes you might need to move slowly through a window. You can move the contents of a window one windowful at a time by clicking in the scroll bar on either side of the scroll box.

 **Empty Window?**   Don't worry if text, graphics, or icons don't appear in a window. Use the scroll bar to bring the text, graphics, or icons into view.

## SIZING A WINDOW WITH MAXIMIZE, MINIMIZE, AND RESTORE

You may want to increase the size of a window to see its full contents, or you may want to decrease a window's size (even down to button form on the taskbar) to make room for other windows. One way to resize a window is to use the Maximize, Minimize, and Restore commands. If you use the mouse, you will use the Maximize, Minimize, and Restore buttons located on the right side of the window's title bar. If you use the keyboard, you can use the Maximize, Minimize, and Restore menu commands on the Control menu. The following list defines the purpose of each of these buttons and commands:

- Select the Maximize button or command to enlarge the window to its maximum size.

- Select the Minimize button or command to reduce the window to a button on the taskbar.

- Select the Restore button or command to return a window to the size it was before it was maximized. (The Restore button and command are available only after a window has been maximized.)

Figure 2.3 shows the My Computer window maximized to full-screen size. At full size, the Minimize and Restore buttons are available. At any other size, you see the Maximize button instead of the Restore button.

Minimize button

Restore
button

FIGURE 2.3    The My Computer window maximized to full-screen
size.

To maximize, minimize, or restore a window with the mouse,
click the appropriate button. To maximize, minimize, or restore a
window with the keyboard, follow these steps:

1. Press **Alt+Spacebar** (for an application window) or
   **Alt+–** (for a document window) to open the window's
   Control menu.

2. Select the Restore, Minimize, or Maximize command
   from the menu.

# SIZING A WINDOW'S BORDERS

At some point, you may need a window to be a particular size to suit your needs. If so, simply drag the window border to change the size of the window.

To use the mouse, follow these steps:

1. Place the mouse pointer on the portion of the border (vertical, horizontal, or corner) that you want to resize. When the mouse pointer is positioned correctly, it changes into one of the shapes described here:

   The vertical double-headed arrow appears when you position the mouse pointer over the top or bottom window border. It enables you to resize the window's height by dragging the border up or down.

   The horizontal double-headed arrow appears when you position the mouse pointer over either side of the window border. It enables you to resize the window's width by dragging the border left or right.

   The diagonal double-headed arrow appears when you position the mouse pointer over any of the four corners of the window border. It enables you to resize the window's height and width proportionally by dragging the corner diagonally.

2. Press the mouse button and drag the border. A faint line appears, indicating where the border will be when you release the mouse button.

3. Once the border is in the desired location, release the mouse button. The window is resized.

To resize a window using the keyboard, follow these steps:

1. Press **Alt+Spacebar** (for an application window) or **Alt+ −** (for a document window) to open the window's Control menu.

2. Press **S** to choose the Size command. The pointer becomes a four-headed arrow.

3. Use the arrow keys to move the pointer to the border or corner you want to resize. The mouse pointer turns into a different shape.

4. With the pointer on the border or corner, press the arrow keys to resize the window. A faint line appears showing the new border location.

5. When the faint line appears to be the size you want, press **Enter**. To cancel the operation, press **Esc**.

## MOVING A WINDOW

When you start working with multiple windows, moving a window becomes as important as sizing one. For example, you may need to move one or more windows to make room for other work on your desktop.

You can move a window with the mouse or keyboard. To move a window using the mouse, point at the window's title bar, press and hold the left mouse button, and drag it to a new location. To use the keyboard, follow these steps:

1. Press **Alt+Spacebar** (for an application window) or **Alt+ −** (for a document window) to open the window's Control menu.

2. Press **M** to choose the Move command. The pointer changes to a four-headed arrow.

3. Use the arrow keys to move the window to a new location.

4. When the window is located where you want it, press **Enter.** To cancel the operation and return the window to its original location, press **Esc.**

# CLOSING A WINDOW

When you're finished working with a window, you should close it. This can help speed up Windows, conserve memory, and keep your desktop from becoming cluttered.

To close a window with the mouse:

1. Click on the Control menu icon to display the Control menu.

2. Choose (click) the Close command to close the window.

 **TIP** **Quickie Close** To quickly close a window with the mouse, click on the Close button.

If you'd rather use the keyboard, select the window you want to close and press **Alt+F4.**

In this lesson, you learned how to use windows. In the next lesson, you'll learn how to use menus.

# USING MENUS

*In this lesson, you learn how to select and open menus, choose menu commands, and read a menu.*

## WHAT IS A MENU?

A *menu* is a group of related commands that tells Windows 95 what you want to do. Menu commands are organized in logical groups. For example, all the commands related to starting your work in Windows 95 are on the Start menu. The names of the available menus appear in the Start menu or on the menu bar in an application window.

In telling you to choose commands from a pull-down menu, this book uses the format *menu title, menu command*. For example, the statement "choose File, Properties" means to "open the File menu and select the Properties command."

**Pull-Down Menu**   A menu that appears to "pull-down" from the menu bar. You access the menu by clicking on its name in the menu bar.

### CHOOSING MENU COMMANDS WITH THE MOUSE

To choose a menu command with the mouse, click on the menu title in the menu bar. The menu opens to display the available commands. To choose a particular command, simply click on it. For example, to see the Help options available for My Computer, click the Help menu title in the My Computer menu bar. The Help menu appears (see Figure 3.1). You can make the menu disappear by clicking anywhere outside of it.

FIGURE 3.1    The Help menu.

To see the available topics from the Help facility, choose the Help Topics command, and a Help window appears. (Remember, to close this or any window, click the Close button.) For more information on using Help, refer to Lesson 5.

## CHOOSING MENU COMMANDS USING THE KEYBOARD

You can also select menus and menu commands with the keyboard. To do so, press **Alt** to activate the menu bar of the active window. The first menu title becomes highlighted, indicating that the menu bar is active. With the menu bar active, you can select a menu using either of two methods:

- Use the arrow keys to highlight the menu title you want, and then press **Enter**.

- Press the key that corresponds to the underlined letter of the menu. For example, to open the Help menu, press **H**.

Once the menu is open, you select a command from the menu using the same techniques you used to open the menu. Highlight the command with the arrow keys and press **Enter**, or press the key that corresponds to the underlined letter to select the command you want.

To open the Control menu with the keyboard, press **Alt+Spacebar** in an application window (such as Microsoft Word or My Computer), or press **Alt+–** (hyphen) in a document. Then highlight your selection using the arrow keys and press **Enter**, or press the key that corresponds to the underlined letter of the command. To close the Control menu (or any menu for that matter), press **Esc**.

 **Commands, Options, or Selections?**    Commands, menu options, and menu selections all refer to the same thing: items you choose from a menu. Further, commands may be "performed," "executed," or "selected." This simply means that the computer carries out the instructions associated with the command (whether it is to display another menu or perform an operation).

# Reading a Menu

Windows 95's menus (and those of most other Windows applications) contain a number of common elements. For example, *selection letters* (letters that you press to choose a command) appear underlined. Some menu commands list *shortcut keys* that you can use to bypass the menus; shortcut keys are displayed to the right of their associated commands. (Shortcut keys aren't available for every menu option; generally, they are available for such common commands as Open, Save, and Print.) And some commands appear with a right-pointing arrow to the side, which indicates that if you choose the command, another menu will appear with more menu options.

**Unavailable Commands** Some menu commands may appear grayed-out, which means that you cannot currently use them. These commands are only available for use under certain circumstances. For example, you cannot select the Copy command if you have not first selected an object to copy.

Another menu element you will see often is the *ellipsis* (...). An ellipsis appears after a command to indicate that Windows 95 needs more information in order to complete the command. To get that information, Windows 95 displays a *dialog box*. For more on dialog boxes, see Lesson 4.

Figure 3.2 shows a number of these common menu elements.

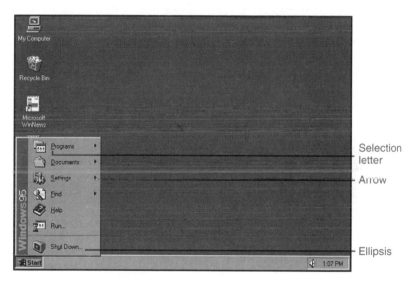

**FIGURE 3.2**    The Start menu.

Another common menu element is the check mark. The check mark indicates that a menu option is currently active. Each time you choose the menu command, the option is turned on or off (like a light switch). When a check mark is present, the option is turned on.

To practice using menu commands, let's suppose you want to shut down Windows 95. (Remember you must shut down Windows before you turn off or restart your computer.) Follow these steps:

1.  Open the Start menu using either the mouse or the keyboard.

2.  Choose Shut Down (notice the ellipsis following the Shut Down command). A dialog box appears.

3.  If you want to shut down Windows 95, click the Yes command button or press **Enter**. To abort the shut down process, click the No command button or press **Esc**.

# USING SHORTCUT KEYS INSTEAD OF MENUS

When you first get started, you'll need to use the menus to view and select commands. However, once you become familiar with Windows 95, you'll probably want to use shortcut keys for commands you use often. Shortcut keys enable you to select a command without using the menus. Shortcut keys generally combine the Alt, Ctrl, or Shift key with a letter key (such as W). If a shortcut key is available, it is listed on the pull-down menu to the right of the command.

For example, Figure 3.3 shows the Edit menu from the My Computer window. Notice that you can choose Edit, Select All to select everything in the window, or you can press the shortcut key **Ctrl+A** to bypass the menu.

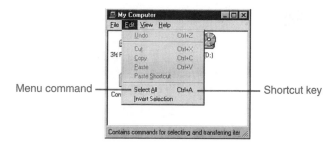

Menu command ——— Shortcut key

**FIGURE 3.3** Use shortcut keys to bypass menus.

In this lesson, you learned how to use menus. In the next lesson, you'll learn how to use dialog boxes.

# 4 LESSON

# USING DIALOG BOXES

*In this lesson, you learn how to use the various dialog box components.*

## WHAT IS A DIALOG BOX?

Windows 95 uses *dialog boxes* to exchange information with you. As you learned in Lesson 3, a menu command followed by an ellipsis (...) indicates that when you select the command, a dialog box will appear asking you for the information the program needs to complete the operation.

Windows 95 also displays dialog boxes to give you information. For example, Windows 95 might display a dialog box to warn you about a problem (for example, to say **File already exists, Overwrite?**) or to confirm that an operation should take place (for example, to confirm that you're ready to shut down).

## USING THE COMPONENTS OF A DIALOG BOX

Dialog boxes vary in complexity. Some simply ask you to confirm an operation before it is executed (in which case you select OK to confirm the operation or Cancel to abort it). On the other hand, some dialog boxes are quite complex, asking you to specify several options.

The following list briefly explains the components of a dialog box, and the rest of the lesson describes the components and how to use them in greater detail.

**Text box**   A text box provides you with a place to type an entry, such as a name for a file you want to save or a path (drive and directory) you want to use to find a specific file.

**List box**   A list box presents a list of possible choices from which you can choose. Scroll bars often accompany a list box so you can scroll through the list. In addition, a text box is sometimes associated with a list box: the list item that you select appears in the text box associated with the list.

**Drop-down list box**   This box is a single-line list box with a down-arrow button to the right of it. When you click on the arrow, the drop-down list box opens to display a list of choices.

**Option buttons**   Option buttons present a group of re-lated choices from which you can choose only one. Simply click on the option button you want to select, and all others become deselected.

**Check boxes**   Check boxes present a single option or group of related options. A check mark appears in the box next to an option to indicate that it is active.

**Command buttons**   When selected, command buttons carry out the command displayed on the button (Open, Help, Quit, Cancel, OK, and so on). If there is an ellipsis on the button (such as Options...), choosing it will open an-other dialog box.

**Tabs**   Tabs represent multiple sections of a dialog box. Only one tab is displayed at a time, and each tab contains related options. Choosing a tab changes the options that appear in the dialog box.

## USING TEXT BOXES

You use a text box to enter the information that Windows 95 needs to complete a command. This information is usually a file name or directory name. Figure 4.1 shows a text box and list boxes in the Open dialog box (accessed from the Windows 95 WordPad File menu).

Text box

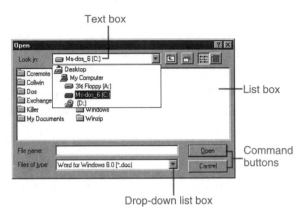

List box

Command buttons

Drop-down list box

**Figure 4.1**   A text box and list boxes in the Open dialog box.

To activate a text box using the mouse, simply click in the text box. Notice that the insertion point (the flashing vertical line that indicates where the text you type will appear) appears in the active text box.

To activate a text box using the keyboard, press **Alt+*selection letter***. For example, to activate the File Name text box shown in Figure 4.1, press Alt+N.

Once you have activated a text box and typed text into it, you can use several keys to edit the text. Table 4.1 outlines these keys.

**Table 4.1   Editing Keys for Text Boxes**

| Key | Description |
| --- | --- |
| Delete | Deletes the character to the right of the insertion point. |
| Backspace | Erases the character to the left of the insertion point. |
| End | Moves the insertion point to the end of the line. |

| Key | Description |
|---|---|
| Home | Moves the insertion point to the beginning of the line. |
| Arrow keys | Move the insertion point one character in the direction of the arrow. |
| Shift+End | Selects the text from the insertion point to the end of the line. |
| Shift+Home | Selects the text from the insertion point to the beginning of the line. |
| Shift+Arrow key | Selects the next character in the direction of the arrow. |
| Ctrl+C | Copies selected text to the Clipboard. |
| Ctrl+V | Pastes selected text from the Clipboard. |

## Using List Boxes

You use a list box to make a selection from a list of available options. For example, you use the Look In list box in the Open dialog box (see Figure 4.1) to select a file to open.

To select an item from a list box using the mouse, click on the appropriate list item. In the Look In list box, notice that the item you select is automatically displayed in the linked text box above the list box. Click Open or press **Enter** to accept the selection; click Cancel or press **Esc** to close the dialog box without making the selection.

To select an item from a list box using the keyboard:

1. Press **Alt+*selection letter*** to activate the list box. For example, to activate the Look In list box displayed in Figure 4.1, press **Alt+I**. Press the Tab key to move to the list.

2. Press the up and down arrow keys or **PageUp** and **PageDown** to move through the list. Each list item appears highlighted as you come to it.

3. When the item you want is highlighted, press **Enter** to accept the selection and close the dialog box.

To select an item from a drop-down list box using the mouse, open the list box by clicking the down-arrow, and then click the appropriate list item.

To select a drop-down list box item using the keyboard:

1. Press **Alt+***selection letter* to activate the list box.

2. Press the down arrow key to open the drop-down list box.

3. Press the up and down arrow keys or **PageUp** and **PageDown** to scroll through the list.

4. Press **Enter** to make your selection and close the dialog box.

## USING OPTION BUTTONS

Option buttons enable you to make a single choice from a list of possible command options. For example, the Print Range options displayed in Figure 4.2 enable you to choose which pages of your document you want to print. The active option (the All option in Figure 4.2) is indicated by the small filled-in circle.

To select an option button with the mouse, click the circle for the option you want. To use the keyboard, press **Alt+***selection letter* for the option you want. For example, press **Alt+A** to activate the All option.

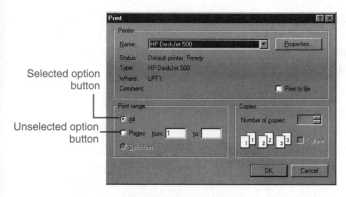

**FIGURE 4.2**    Option buttons in WordPad's Print dialog box.

# USING CHECK BOXES

Command options that you can select (activate) or deselect (deactivate) are usually presented as check boxes. When a check box is selected, a check mark appears in the box, indicating the associated command option is active (see Figure 4.3).

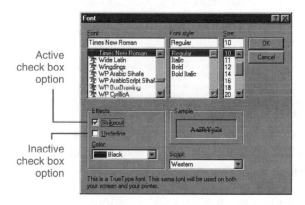

**FIGURE 4.3**    Check boxes in WordPad's Font dialog box.

To select or deselect a check box with the mouse, click on its box. Using the keyboard, press **Alt+*selection letter*** to select or deselect a check box. For example, press **Alt+K** to activate the Strikeout option shown in Figure 4.3.

## USING COMMAND BUTTONS

You use command buttons to perform operations. To select command buttons with the mouse, simply click the appropriate command button. Figure 4.3 shows two common command buttons: OK and Cancel. Select the OK command button to accept the information you have entered or to verify an action and close the dialog box. (Pressing Enter is equivalent to selecting the OK button.) Select the Cancel command button to leave the dialog box without executing the information you provided in the dialog box. (Pressing Esc is the keyboard equivalent to selecting the Cancel button.)

**Accidents Happen**  If you accidentally select the Cancel command button, don't worry. You can always reenter the dialog box and continue. Be careful when you select OK, however: the instructions you have entered in the dialog box will be executed.

## USING TABS

Windows 95 uses tabs to organize the options in a dialog box into categories (like a set of index dividers in a notebook). Tabs appear across the top of some dialog boxes, and each tabbed section contains a different set of options. Click on a tab to go to that area of the dialog box and access that tab's set of options. Figure 4.4 shows three tabs.

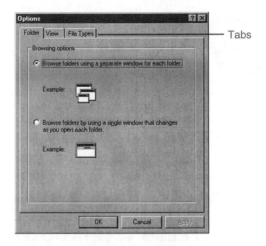

**FIGURE 4.4**   The Folder tab, the View tab, and the File Types tab in My Computer's Options dialog box.

In this lesson, you learned how to use the different components of dialog boxes. In the next lesson, you'll learn how to use Windows 95's Help system.

# USING WINDOWS 95 HELP

*In this lesson, you learn how to get help, use Help's shortcut buttons, and use the What's This? feature.*

## GETTING HELP IN WINDOWS 95

Windows 95 offers several ways to get *online help*, instant on-screen help for menu commands or other tools. Online help is Help information that appears in its own window whenever you request it. The Help feature is organized like a reference book with three tabs: Contents, Index, and Find. The Contents and Index features show you step by step how to use commands and functions and how to perform operations in Windows 95's applications and accessories. The Find feature enables you to search for specific words and phrases in a Help topic. Whether you use the keyboard or the mouse to access Help, help information is always available at your fingertips. If you do not know or cannot remember how to perform some task, you can use Windows 95's Help system to tell you how.

To get help on common tasks, follow these steps:

1. Click the Start button. The Start menu appears.

2. Choose Help from the Start menu. The Help Topics: Windows Help window appears, showing a list of Help topics.

3. Click the Contents tab to browse through the Help topics listed in the Help window, or click the Index tab to search for a specific Help topic. You can click the Find tab to search for specific words or phrases in a Help topic.

**Fast Help**   You can press F1 at any time to access the Help system from within a program.

**New and Improved Help**   The Help systems in Windows 3.1 and Windows 95 are organized differently. Whereas Windows 3.1 is divided into the categories Contents, Search, and Glossary, Windows 95 is divided into the categories Contents, Index, and Find. In addition, you no longer have to scroll through the Help window to find a topic because the list of Help topics is short: they all fit on one small screen.

## USING THE CONTENTS FEATURE

You can get help with common tasks using Help's Contents feature. The Contents feature displays the top level groups of information covered in Help, such as How To and Tips and Tricks. When you open a major group, a list of main topics appears. As you can see in Figure 5.1, both the major groups and the main topics in each group are represented by book icons, and subtopics are represented by page icons (with a question mark). You can simply select a book to see a list of the subtopics.

Follow these steps to use Help's Contents feature.

1. Click the main group that contains the Help topic you want to open. The group's name becomes highlighted.

2. Click the Open button to open the group. A list of chapters in that group appears.

3. Click the chapter that contains the Help topic you want to open. The chapter name becomes highlighted.

4. Click the Open button to open the chapter. A list of subtopics appears below the open chapter.

5. Click the subtopic you want to display and click the Display button that appears. A window appears, displaying the Help information.

6. After you read the explanation, click the Close button in the Help window's title bar to close the Windows Help window.

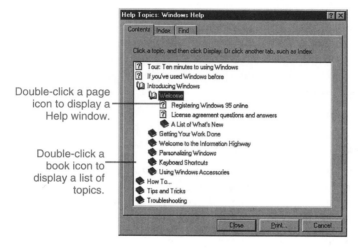

**FIGURE 5.1**   The Help Topics: Windows Help window.

If you want to print the list of Help topics in the Help Topics: Windows Help window, click the Print button at the bottom of the window. The Print dialog box appears. Click the OK button to print the list of help topics and subtopics.

## USING THE INDEX FEATURE

Help's Index feature provides a list of Help topics arranged alphabetically in the Index list box. In Figure 5.2, for example, the "copying" topic appears in the topic text box and is highlighted in the topic list. In some cases, Windows 95 displays more than one related topic in the topic list, and you can select which topic you need more information on. The Index is especially useful when you cannot find a particular Help topic in Help Contents' list of topics.

To use the Help Index, follow these steps:

1. Click the Index tab in the Windows Help window. The Index options are displayed.

2. Type a topic in the text box. This enters the topic for which you want to search and scrolls to the first entry that matches the word you typed. That topic appears highlighted in the topic list.

3. Click on a subtopic, if necessary. Then click the Display button, and Windows 95 displays the selected Help topic information in a Windows Help window.

4. When you are finished reading the Help information, click the Close button to close the Windows Help window.

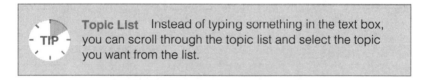

**Topic List**   Instead of typing something in the text box, you can scroll through the topic list and select the topic you want from the list.

FIGURE 5.2   The Index tab in the Windows Help window.

## USING THE FIND FEATURE

You can search for specific words and phrases in a Help topic instead of searching for a Help topic by category. First, however, you have to instruct Windows to create a list that contains every word from your Help files. (You only have to create the word list once.) Then you can search for words and phrases similar to existing words and phrases in a Help topic. In Figure 5.3, for example, the word "activated" appears in the text box and is highlighted in the word list. The Find feature is especially useful when you cannot find a particular help topic in Help Contents' or Index's list of topics.

To build a word list, follow these steps:

1. Click the Find tab in the Windows Help dialog box. The dialog box that appears gives an explanation of the Find feature and gives you these options: Minimize database size, Maximize search capabilities, and Customize search capabilities.

2. Choose the Minimize Database Size option to create a short word list, choose the Maximize Search Capabilities option to create a long word list, or choose the Customize Search Capabilities option to create a shorter word list if you have limited disk space.

3. Click the Next button to continue.

4. Click the Finish button to create the word list.

After Windows creates the word list, the Find tab contains a text box, a word list, and a topic list.

To search for words or a phrase in a Help topic:

1. Type the word you want to find in the first text box at the top of the dialog box. This enters the word for which you want to search and scrolls to the first entry that matches the word you typed. The word appears highlighted in the word list.

2. Click on another word in the word list to narrow the search if necessary.

3. Click on a topic in the topic list, and then click on the Display button. Windows 95 displays the selected Help topic information in a Windows Help window.

4. When you are finished reading the Help information, click the Close button to close the Windows Help window.

Word text box —
Word list box—
Topic list box —

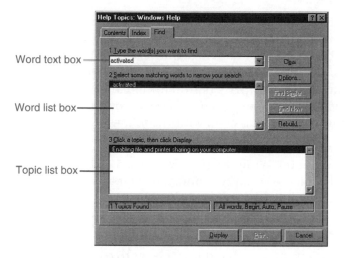

FIGURE 5.3   The Find tab in the Windows Help window.

 **TIP**   **Topic List**   Instead of typing something in the text box, you can scroll through the word list and select the word you want from the list. If you want to find words similar to the words in a Help topic, click the Find Similar button.

**Accidents Happen**    If you don't want to use the first list that Windows created, don't worry. You can rebuild that list to include more words or to exclude words. Simply click the Rebuild button and choose a word list option to recreate the word list.

# USING HELP WINDOWS

When you display any Windows Help option, a button bar is displayed at the top of the Help window, and it always remains visible. This button bar includes three buttons: Help Topics, Back, and Options. Click the Help Topics button to return to Help's table of contents. Click the Back button to close the current Windows Help window and return to the preceding one. Click the Options button to display a menu with the following commands:

**Annotate**    Select this command if you want to add notes to the text in the Windows Help window. A dialog box appears, in which you can type and save your text. When you save the annotation, a green paper clip appears to the right of the Help topic to indicate that it has an annotation. Click the paper clip to view the annotation.

**Copy**    Select this command if you want to copy Help text to the Clipboard.

**Print Topic**    Select this command to display the Print dialog box. Then click the OK button to print the topic using the current printer settings, or click the Properties button to change printer settings.

**Font**    Select this command to change the size of the font displayed in the Windows Help window. When you select this command, another menu appears from which you can select Small, Normal, or Large. A check mark indicates the current size.

**Keep Help on Top**    Select this command if you want the Windows Help window to always be in the foreground of your screen. When you select this command, another menu appears from which you can select Default, On Top, or Not On Top. A check mark indicates the current selection.

**Use System Colors**    Select this command if you want Windows to use regular system colors for Help windows. When you select this command, a dialog box appears, informing you that you must restart Help for the color change to take effect. Choose Yes to close Help or choose No to return to the Windows Help window.

Help windows often display shortcut buttons as well. Using shortcut buttons, you can jump to the area of Windows 95 to which the Help information refers. For example, suppose you're reading a Help topic that contains information on how to change the wallpaper on the desktop (see Figure 5.4). You click the shortcut button (the button with an arrow that curves up and to the left) to jump to the Control Panel's Properties for Display dialog box from within Help. There you can make the necessary changes and get on with your work.

To use a shortcut button, simply click on it, and you're immediately taken to that area of Windows 95.

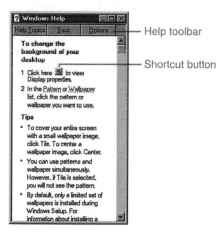

**FIGURE 5.4**    The shortcut button in the Help window.

# USING THE WHAT'S THIS? FEATURE

The What's This? feature provides a handy way of getting more information about dialog box options. You activate this feature by selecting the ? icon, which appears on the right side of the title bar in all Windows 95 dialog boxes.

The following steps tell you how to use the What's This feature to display a description of any option in a Windows 95 dialog box.

1. Click the ? icon in the upper-right corner of the Windows 95 dialog box. A large question mark appears next to the mouse pointer.

2. Click on any option in the dialog box. Windows 95 displays a box containing a short description of the item you selected.

3. When you are finished reading the Help information, click anywhere on the screen to close the Help box.

 **TIP** **Quick Description** If you right-click on an option in a dialog box, a shortcut menu appears displaying one menu command: What's This? Click on What's This? to view a description of the option.

In this lesson, you learned how to access Windows 95's Help system. In the next lesson, you'll learn how to shut down Windows 95.

# Shutting Down Windows 95

*In this lesson, you learn the various ways you can shut down and restart Windows 95.*

You can shut down Windows 95 in one of three ways: you can shut down the computer, you can restart the computer, or you can restart the computer in MS-DOS mode. The following sections cover each of these methods.

## Shutting Down the Computer

Before you shut down Windows 95, you should save any work you have in progress and close any open DOS applications so you won't lose any data. In most Windows applications, you choose File, Save to save a document, and then choose File, Exit to exit the application. If you don't save your data and close open applications, when you choose Shut Down, Windows closes each application for you and asks you to confirm saving each file.

To shut down the computer:

1. Click the Start button. The Start menu appears.

2. Choose Shut Down from the Start menu. The Shut Down Windows dialog box appears (see Figure 6.1), displaying a list of shut down options.

3. Choose the Shut down the computer? option and choose Yes. Windows 95 prompts you to turn off your computer.

4. Turn off your computer, or press **Ctrl+Alt+Del** to restart it.

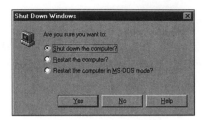

**FIGURE 6.1**    The Shut Down Windows dialog box.

 **Shutting Down**   If you close all open documents and applications and return to the Windows 95 desktop, you can press **Alt+F4** to shut down the computer.

Because you can work with several documents and applications at one time, you may get carried away and forget to save a document before you shut down. Fear not: Windows 95 protects you from losing your data. For example, if you're working on a WordPad document and try to shut down Windows 95 without saving the document, the dialog box shown in Figure 6.2 appears, prompting you to save your changes.

**FIGURE 6.2**    WordPad prompts you to save changes before shutting down.

Select Yes to save the changes, select No to discard any changes you made, or select Cancel to cancel the shut down command altogether.

**Forget to Save?** This message is your only warning. If you accidentally respond No to saving changes, the changes you made in the document are lost.

# RESTARTING THE COMPUTER

When you experience system problems, you can restart the computer to clear up any problems you have encountered. To do so, follow these steps:

1.  Click the Start button. The Start menu appears.

2.  Choose Shut Down from the Start menu. The Shut Down Windows dialog box appears (see Figure 6.1), displaying a list of shut down options.

3.  Choose the Restart the computer? option and choose Yes. Windows 95 restarts your computer. If you're on a network, Windows asks you to log in.

 **Restarting the Computer** Choosing the Restart the computer? option in Windows 95's Shut Down Windows dialog box is different from pressing **Ctrl+Alt+Delete**. If you press **Ctrl+Alt+Delete** in Windows 95, the Close Program dialog box appears, in which you can end selected tasks or choose the Shut Down option.

# RESTARTING THE COMPUTER IN MS-DOS MODE

If you are using DOS programs and want to work in MS-DOS mode, you might not want to exit Windows 95 temporarily by choosing the MS-DOS Prompt program in the Programs menu. Instead, you can shut down Windows 95 and restart your computer in MS-DOS mode. The benefit of running in MS-DOS mode is that multitasking can't take place like it can when you run a DOS application in Windows. Some DOS games and other DOS applications require exclusive use of the CPU and other resources and won't operate properly—or at all—within Windows. All programs don't run faster, but you may notice a small increase in speed in some DOS applications.

Before restarting your computer, make sure you save your work and close any open applications. Then follow these steps:

1. Click the Start button. The Start menu appears.

2. Choose Shut Down from the Start menu. The Shut Down Windows dialog box appears (see Figure 6.1), displaying a list of shut down options.

3. Choose the Restart the computer in MS-DOS mode option and then choose Yes. Your computer is restarted, and the MS-DOS prompt appears on-screen.

4. To return to Windows, type EXIT at the MS-DOS prompt and press **Enter**. The computer restarts.

## CLOSING ALL PROGRAMS AND LOGGING ON AS A DIFFERENT USER

If you're on a network, you can also shut down Windows 95 by logging off, but leaving Windows 95 running. This feature is useful when you no longer want to work in Windows 95, but other users want to use your computer and work in Windows 95. To log off, choose the Close all programs and log on as a different user option in the Shut Down Windows dialog box. Choose Yes, and then enter your network password.

 **Logoff**   The Logoff feature in Windows 95 is not available in Windows 3.1 unless you're running Windows for Workgroups.

In this lesson, you learned how to shut down Windows. In the next lesson, you'll learn how to start and exit applications.

# STARTING AND EXITING APPLICATIONS

*In this lesson, you learn how to start Windows
applications, use a document window, and exit Windows applications.*

## STARTING WINDOWS APPLICATIONS

A Windows application is a program designed to take advantage
of the *graphical user interface (GUI)* built into Windows 95. By defi-
nition, a GUI provides a common interface between you and your
programs that enables you to use the same procedures to execute
commands in most compatible applications. In the context of this
lesson, that means that you can start (and exit) most Windows
applications using the same procedures. If you are using a non-
Windows (DOS) application through Windows 95, you will need
to consult that application's manual to learn how to start and
exit.

There are several ways to start a Windows application. This lesson
discusses four of those ways. Lesson 20, "Customizing the Desktop," explains how you can create shortcuts and rearrange the
Start menu to make starting an application even easier.

### USING THE PROGRAMS MENU

To start an application from the Programs menu using the mouse,
follow these steps:

1. Click the Start button. The Start menu appears.

2. Choose Programs from the Start menu. The Programs
   menu appears.

3. Click the program folder that contains the program icon for the application you want to use. For example, if you want to use WordPad, open the Accessories folder to access the WordPad program icon (see Figure 7.1).

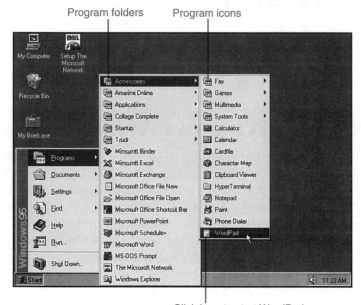

Click here to start WordPad.

FIGURE 7.1   Program icons in the Accessories program folder.

4. Click the program icon for the application you want to start, and the application window appears.

To start an application from the Programs menu using the keyboard, follow these steps:

1. Press **Ctrl+Esc** to access the Start menu.

2. Press **P** to select Programs from the Start menu. The Programs menu appears.

3. Use the arrow keys to highlight the program folder that contains the program item for the application you want to use. Press **Enter** to select the folder.

**4.** Use the arrow keys to highlight the program icon for the application, and press **Enter** to start the application. The application window appears.

## STARTING AN APPLICATION WHEN YOU START WINDOWS

If you have a particular program that you use every day, you can add it to the Startup folder, and Windows will start it every time you start Windows. To learn how to add a program to the Startup folder, see Lesson 20, "Customizing the Desktop." To view the applications in the Startup folder, click on the Start button, select Programs, and select Startup.

 **Startup**   The Startup folder functions much the same way the Startup program group does in Windows 3.1's Program Manager.

## STARTING AN APPLICATION FROM A DOCUMENT

There are several ways that you can start an application from a document. You can start an application from the Documents list by following these steps:

**1.** Click the Start button. The Start menu appears.

**2.** Click on Documents, and the Documents list appears, displaying the names of the 15 documents you've used most recently.

**3.** Click on the document you want. Windows opens the application in which the document was created and then opens the document.

You can also open a document from the Explorer or My Computer by simply double-clicking on the document. Windows immediately starts the application in which the document was created and opens the document.

## USING THE RUN COMMAND

You can use the Run command to start applications that you use infrequently and that are not listed in the Programs menu. Or you might start a program with the Run command so you can enter command parameters or options that change the way the application starts. For example, in most word processing programs, if you start the program using the Run command, you can add a parameter that tells the application to open a specific file automatically upon startup.

 **What Are Your Options?**   Check the documentation that comes with your software to find out about the available start-up options. You may want to jot down special start-up commands you plan to use often.

To use the Run command, follow these steps:

1. Click the Start Button. The Start menu appears.

2. Choose Run from the Start menu. The Run dialog box appears (see Figure 7.2).

3. Type the required command in the Open text box. Figure 7.2 displays the command that opens WordPerfect for Windows (wpwin), with a file (report.wpp) open and ready to edit. If necessary, you can include any program not in the path statement (drive and folder)—usually just the Windows folder.

4. When the command is complete, select OK. (If you decide not to use the Run command, select Cancel.)

 **Can't Remember the Command?**   If you don't remember the command that runs the application, click the Browse button in the Run dialog box. In the Browse dialog box that appears, choose the files you want to run.

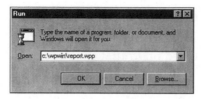

**FIGURE 7.2**   You can load a program and a document file using the Run command.

# WORKING WITH DOCUMENT WINDOWS

When you use certain applications with Windows 95, you will create documents. For example, any letter you write in WordPerfect for Windows or any drawing you create in Windows 95's Paint program is contained in a document. These documents are sometimes called *files* or *document files*. When you are working on a document, it appears in a window.

When you start up an application, the application automatically creates a window for a new document. In most applications, you can create another document window by choosing the File, New command from that application's menu bar. The application creates a new window so you can start a new document, but any other document you might have been working on remains available. (If you're using WordPad, you can open only one document at a time. However you can have multiple WordPad windows open simultaneously.)

When you are finished with a document, always save your changes by choosing File, Save, and then close the document window by choosing File, Close or simply by double-clicking on the document window's Control menu icon. This ensures that the document will not be lost or damaged accidentally. When you close a document window, the application remains open. The next section explains how to close the document window(s) and exit the application.

# EXITING WINDOWS APPLICATIONS

Before you exit an application, be sure to save and close any documents you have worked on in that application (using the commands on the File menu).

 **Forget to Save Your Changes?** If you attempt to close a document window or exit an application without saving your changes, Windows 95 will ask you if you want to save before closing. To save any changes, click Yes; to exit without saving, click No; to remain in the application, click Cancel.

Once you have saved and closed all document files, you can exit a Windows application using any of the following four methods.

- To exit an application using its Control menu icon (the icon in the upper-left corner of the application window), double-click the Control menu icon. If you prefer to use the keyboard, press **Alt+Spacebar** to open the application's Control menu and press **C** to choose the Close command.

- To exit an application using its Close button, click the Close button (the button with an X on the right end of the application's title bar).

- To exit an application using the menus, choose File, Exit. You can click on the commands with the mouse, or you can press **Alt+F** to open the File menu and press **X** to select Exit.

- The quickest way to exit is to use the shortcut key. Press **Alt+F4**, and you're on your way.

**Exit Quickly**   You can right-click on the application's button on the taskbar to display the shortcut menu. Then choose Close to close the application.

**Exiting Windows Applications**   Exiting Windows applications in Windows 95 and Windows 3.1 is handled the same way except that the Control menus look different, and application windows in Windows 3.1 do not have a Close button.

In this lesson, you learned how to start applications, use a document window, and exit applications. In the next lesson, you'll learn how to work with multiple windows.

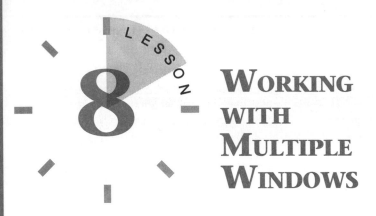

# WORKING WITH MULTIPLE WINDOWS

*In this lesson, you learn how to arrange windows, move between windows in the same application, and move between applications.*

In Windows 95, you can use more than one application at a time, and in each Windows application, you can work with multiple document windows. As you can imagine, opening multiple applications with multiple windows can make your desktop pretty cluttered. That's why it's important that you know how to manipulate and switch between windows. The following sections explain how to do just that.

## ARRANGING WINDOWS

When you have multiple windows open, some windows are inevitably hidden by others, which makes the screen confusing. You can use the commands on the taskbar's shortcut menu (which you access by right-clicking on the taskbar) to arrange windows.

### CASCADING WINDOWS

A good way to get control of a confusing desktop is to right-click a blank area on the taskbar and choose the Cascade command from the shortcut menu. When you choose this command, Windows lays all the open windows on top of each other so that the title bar of each is visible. Figure 8.1 shows the resulting cascaded window arrangement. To access any window that's not on the top, simply click on its title bar.

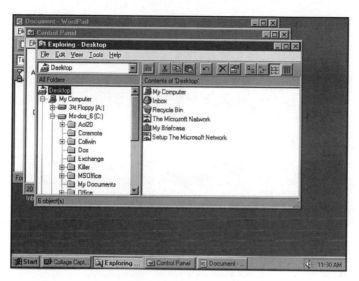

**FIGURE 8.1** Cascaded windows.

## TILING WINDOWS

If you need to see all of your open windows at the same time, use the Tile command on the shortcut menu. When you choose this command, Windows resizes and moves each open window so that they appear side by side horizontally or vertically. Right-click a blank area on the taskbar and choose the Tile Horizontally command from the shortcut menu to create an arrangement similar to that shown in Figure 8.2. To arrange the windows in a vertically tiled arrangement (as shown in Figure 8.3), right-click a blank area on the taskbar and choose the Tile Vertically command. If you want to minimize all the windows at once, right-click a blank area on the taskbar and choose Minimize All Windows. The opened windows disappear from the desktop, but the application buttons remain visible on the taskbar.

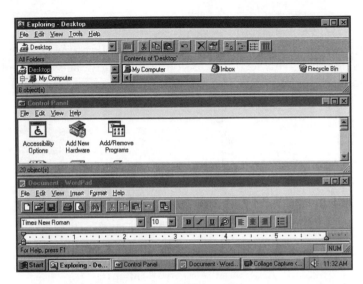

FIGURE 8.2    Horizontally tiled windows.

FIGURE 8.3    Vertically tiled windows.

# MOVING BETWEEN APPLICATIONS

Windows 95 enables you to have multiple applications open at the same time. This section tells you how to move between applications using the taskbar.

**Moving Between Applications** The Task List in Windows 3.1 has been replaced by the taskbar in Windows 95. In Windows 95, when you press **Alt+Tab** to switch to a different application, the icons and application names of all open windows appear in one dialog box. In Windows 3.1, you have to cycle through all the open applications until you get to the one you want.

The taskbar is a button bar that appears at the bottom of your screen by default. Each button on the taskbar represents an open window that's either in the active application or in another application. The taskbar button of the currently active application looks like it's pressed in.

To quickly switch between applications using the taskbar, simply click on the button for the application to which you want to switch. Windows 95 immediately takes you to the application. Figure 8.4 shows two applications represented on the taskbar.

**Bypass the Taskbar** Press and hold the **Alt** key and press the **Tab** key (continue to hold down **Alt**), and a dialog box appears displaying the icons and application names of all open applications. Each time you press **Tab**, a new (open) application is selected, and a border appears around the selected icon. When the application you want is selected, release the Alt key, and Windows 95 switches you to that application. If (while the dialog box is still on-screen) you decide you don't want to switch to that application, press **Esc** and release the Alt key.

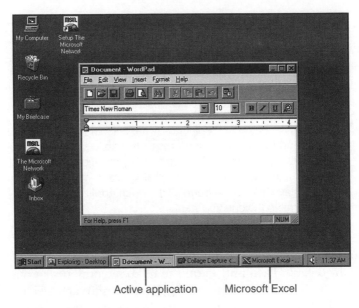

Active application    Microsoft Excel

FIGURE 8.4    The taskbar buttons.

# MOVING BETWEEN WINDOWS IN THE SAME APPLICATION

As I said earlier, in addition to working in multiple applications in Windows 95, you also can open multiple windows within an application. Moving to a new window means you are changing the window that is *active*. If you are using a mouse, you can move to a window by clicking on any part of it. When you do, the title bar becomes highlighted, and you can work in the window. To move to the next window using the keyboard, press **Ctrl+F6**; to move to the previous window, press **Ctrl+Shift+F6**. Figure 8.5 shows Microsoft Word with three open documents arranged horizontally.

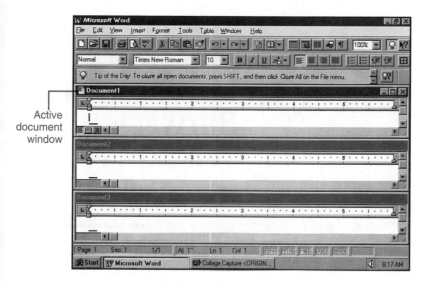

Active
document
window

**FIGURE 8.5**    Three open documents in Microsoft Word.

**Active Window**    The window currently in use. You can tell which window is active because its title bar is highlighted.

**Moving Between Windows**    In Windows 3.1 and Windows 95, you can also use the Window menu to move between windows in the same application.

In this lesson, you learned how to arrange windows, switch between open applications, and switch between windows in the same application. In the next lesson, you'll learn how to copy and move information between windows.

# COPYING AND MOVING INFORMATION BETWEEN WINDOWS

*In this lesson, you learn about the Clipboard and how to copy and move information between windows.*

## WHAT IS THE CLIPBOARD?

One of the handiest features of the Windows 95 environment is its capability to copy or move information (both text and graphics) from one window to another. This includes windows (documents) in the same applications, as well as those in different applications. When you copy or cut information, Windows places it in a storage area called the *Clipboard*.

The Clipboard holds only the information most recently copied or cut. When you copy or cut something else, it replaces anything that was previously on the Clipboard.

 **Copy and Cut** When you *copy* information, the application copies it to the Clipboard without disturbing the original. When you *cut* information, the application removes it from its original location and places it on the Clipboard.

**Paste**   When you *paste* data, the application inserts the information that's on the Clipboard in the location you specify, but the copy on the Clipboard remains intact (so you can use it again, if necessary).

You can see the contents of the Clipboard at any time by following these steps:

1. Click on the Start button to open the Start menu, and select the Programs menu.

2. From the Programs menu, open the Accessories folder.

3. Click the Clipboard Viewer icon, and the Clipboard Viewer window appears.

4. Click the Maximize button in the Clipboard Viewer window's title bar. The contents of the Clipboard appear in the Clipboard Viewer window. Figure 9.1 shows an address in the Clipboard.

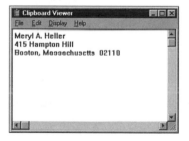

**FIGURE 9.1**   The contents of the Clipboard, as seen through the Clipboard Viewer.

Take a look at the contents of your Clipboard. Unless you have recently copied or cut information, the Clipboard is empty.

**Without a Trace** When you turn off your computer or exit Windows 95, the contents of the Clipboard are lost.

**Clipboard Viewer** The Clipboard Viewer in Windows 95 works the same as it did in Windows 3.1.

# SELECTING TEXT

Before you can copy or cut text, you must identify which text you want copied or cut. This is called *selecting* text. Selected text appears highlighted so you can quickly distinguish it. Figure 9.2 shows selected text in a WordPad document.

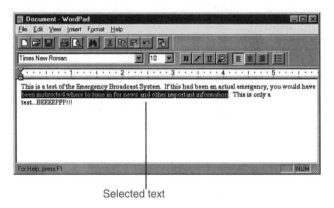

Selected text

**FIGURE 9.2** Selected text in a WordPad document.

To select text with the mouse:

1. Position the mouse pointer just before the first character you want to select.

2. Press and hold the left mouse button, and drag the mouse pointer to the last character you want selected.

3. Release the mouse button. The selected text is highlighted.

To select text with the keyboard:

1. Use the arrow keys to position the insertion point (the blinking vertical line) just before the first character you want to select.

2. Press and hold down the **Shift** key, and use the arrow keys to move the highlight to the last character you want to select.

3. Release all keys, and the selected text appears highlighted.

**Text Selection Shortcuts**    To select a single word using the mouse, double-click on the word. To select text word-by-word (instead of character-by-character) with the keyboard, hold down both the **Shift** and **Ctrl** keys while using the arrow keys.

To get rid of the highlight on the selection (deselect it), click anywhere in the document or press an arrow key.

**Typing over Selected Text**    If you press an alphanumeric key (a letter, number, or other character) while text is highlighted, the text will be deleted and replaced with that character.

# SELECTING GRAPHICS

The procedure for selecting graphics depends on the Windows application you are using. In a word processing program such as WordPad, you select graphics in the same way you select text. In a program like Paint, however, there are special tools for copying and cutting either rectangular or irregular shapes. Since the procedure varies, it is best to refer to the documentation for each application.

## COPYING INFORMATION BETWEEN WINDOWS

Once you have selected the text or graphics, the procedures for copying and pasting are the same in all Windows applications. To copy and paste information between windows of the same application, as well as between windows of different applications, follow these steps:

1. Select the text or graphic to copy (following the instructions earlier in this lesson).

2. Open the Edit menu and choose Copy. A copy of the selected material is placed on the Clipboard; the original selection remains in place.

3. Position the insertion point where you want to insert the selection. (You may need to open another application or document.)

4. Open the Edit menu and choose Paste. Windows copies the selection from the Clipboard to your document. (The original selection remains in its original location, and a copy remains on the Clipboard until you copy or cut something else.)

 **TIP** **Multiple Copies** Because the selected item remains on the Clipboard until you copy or cut again, you can paste information from the Clipboard multiple times. You can also perform other tasks before you paste. (For example, you can leave the selection on the Clipboard while you type new text, and then paste the selection whenever you're ready for it.)

# MOVING INFORMATION BETWEEN WINDOWS

After you have selected text or graphics, the procedures for cutting and pasting are the same in all Windows applications. To cut and paste information between windows of the same application or windows of different applications, follow these steps:

1.  Select the text or graphic to cut (following the instructions earlier in this lesson).

2.  Open the Edit menu and choose Cut. Windows 95 removes the selection from its original location and places it on the Clipboard.

3.  Position the insertion point where you want to insert the selection. (You may need to open another application or document.)

4.  Open the Edit menu and choose Paste. Windows copies the selection from the Clipboard to your document. (A copy remains on the Clipboard until you cut or copy something else.)

 **Copy, Cut, and Paste**   Copying, cutting, and pasting in Windows 95 and Windows 3.1 work the same way.

In this lesson, you learned how to copy and move information between windows. In the next lesson, you'll learn how to browse through the files and folders on different drives.

# 10

# VIEWING DRIVES, FOLDERS, AND FILES WITH MY COMPUTER

*In this lesson, you will learn how to use the My Computer window to examine the contents of your hard, floppy, and CD-ROM drives.*

## UNDERSTANDING DRIVES, FOLDERS, AND FILES

A *drive* is the hardware that seeks, reads, and writes information from and to a disk. A hard disk and its drive are considered one inseparable unit, while a floppy disk can easily be removed from its drive and replaced with a different disk.

Drives are given letter names. For most computers, drives A and B are floppy disk drives, used to store and retrieve data on diskettes. Drive C generally designates the hard disk inside the computer. (Since hard disks and their drives are not easily separated, the terms *disk* and *drive* are often used interchangeably when referring to hard disks.) If the computer has more than one hard disk, or if the hard disk has been divided into multiple partitions (sections), the additional drives are usually labeled D, E, F, and so on.

Because so much information can be stored on a hard disk, hard disks are usually divided into folders. For example, drive C probably has a separate folder for every program you have. Floppy disks can contain folders too, but they usually don't. (Because of their limited capacity, it is easy to keep track of files on a floppy disk without using folders.)

Disk space is not set aside for individual folders; in fact, folders take up hardly any disk space at all. If you think of a disk as a file drawer full of papers, folders are like tabbed file folders used to organize the papers into manageable groups.

**Folders**    What Windows 95 refers to as *folders*, Windows 3.1 refers to as *directories*.

Folders hold files, just as paper file folders hold pieces of paper. Files come in two varieties: *program* (or *executable*) *files* and *document files*. A program file contains the instructions the computer needs to perform. A document file contains a text document that you can read. Regardless of the type of files you're working with, you can use the Windows Explorer to view and control them.

**File Names**    File names in Windows 95 can have up to 255 characters (including spaces) and do not require a file extension; file names in Windows 3.1 can only have up to eight characters and usually have a file extension with a maximum of three characters. To display the file extensions for file names, choose View, Options from the Explorer, My Computer, or any open folder menu. In the Options dialog box, click the View tab, and click the Hide MS-DOS File Extensions for File Types that are Registered check box. The check mark disappears from the check box. Choose OK to display the file extensions.

## VIEWING A DISK'S CONTENTS WITH MY COMPUTER

My Computer enables you to view all files, folders, disk drives, and printers on your computer as icons. This feature is similar to the Windows Explorer.

Using My Computer, you can browse through your computer right from the desktop to find the files you want to open. Follow these steps:

1. Double-click the My Computer icon on the Windows 95 desktop to open the My Computer window. This window contains icons for all the disk drives on your computer as well as the Control Panel folder.

2. Double-click the icon for the drive or folder you want to examine. A window opens that displays that drive's or folder's contents.

3. Select the folder you want to browse by highlighting its icon and choosing File, Open or by double-clicking its icon. You can select additional folders in the same way.

By default, each folder you select opens in its own window, as shown in Figure 10.1. To straighten up the screen and prevent one window from being hidden by the others, you can arrange the windows on the desktop any way you want by dragging each window by its title bar to a new location. For more on arranging multiple windows, refer to Lesson 8.

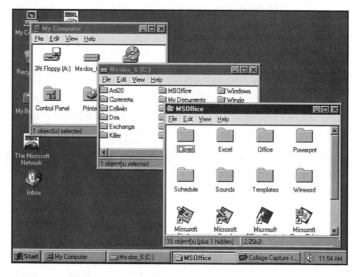

**FIGURE 10.1** Browsing the contents of the A drive and C drive from the My Computer window.

# CHANGING THE MY COMPUTER DISPLAY

By default, when you browse through folders in the My Computer window, Windows displays a separate window for each folder. However, you can control how Windows displays information in the My Computer window. For example, you can set up My Computer as a single window, and you can use the commands on My Computer's View menu to change the size of the icons and how they're displayed.

## SETTING UP A SINGLE WINDOW

If you don't like having all those windows on-screen while you're browsing through your files, you can set Windows 95 to display a single window that changes as you open each folder. Then, no matter how many windows you open, you will only see one window on the desktop at one time.

To set Windows 95 so that you only see a single window as you browse, follow these steps:

1. Open the current window's View menu and select Options. The Options dialog box opens.

2. Click the Folder tab. The Folder options appear (see Figure 10.2).

3. Select the second option (Browse Folders By Using a Single Window that Changes as You Open Each Folder).

4. Click the OK button. As Figure 10.3 shows, Windows 95 places one window on top of another, covering up each open window with the currently open window.

If you want to change back to the default view in which Windows displays multiple browsing windows, repeat the preceding steps but choose the first option (Browse Folders Using a Separate Window for Each Folder) from the Folder tab.

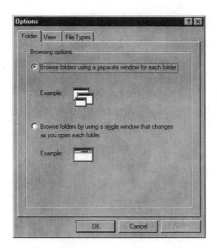

FIGURE 10.2    Browsing options in the Options dialog box.

FIGURE 10.3    The desktop with a single window.

## ARRANGING ICONS

By default, the items in the My Computer window (and any windows you open from this window) appear in Large Icon view. If you have a lot of icons in a window, you may want to open the View menu and choose Small Icons so you can view more icons at a glance. (You can always change back to the default view later by choosing Large Icons from the View menu.)

When arranging a window to suit your needs, you may need to move your icons out of the way by dragging them with the mouse. However, suppose that later you want to return your icons to their original positions. No problem! Choose View, Arrange Icons, Auto Arrange (a check mark appears next to the option when it's selected), and Windows 95 arranges the icons for you automatically. To turn off Auto Arrange, select the same command sequence again; the option is deselected, and the check mark disappears.

**Arranging Icons**   The Auto Arrange command works the same way in Windows 95 that it does in Windows 3.1. Also, in Windows 95 you can use the Arrange Icons command to sort the items in the window by Drive Letter, Type, Size, or Free Space, depending on the view you select. In Windows 3.1, when you select the Arrange Icons command, the icons appear in a window in the order of most usage (for example, programs you use most appear at the top of the window).

To sort the icons in a My Computer window, follow these steps:

1. Open My Computer's View menu.

2. Choose Arrange Icons, and a submenu appears.

3. Choose the sort type you want (Drive Letter, Type, Size, or Free Space). Windows rearranges the icons in the window accordingly.

Another way to clean up the icons in the window is to arrange the icons so that they line up in rows. To do so, choose View, Line Up Icons, and Windows 95 arranges the icons neatly in rows.

# Closing My Computer

To close the My computer window, click the Close button in the upper-right corner of the window. The window shrinks to an icon on the desktop.

In this lesson, you learned how to view the contents of the drives on your computer by using the My Computer window. In the next lesson, you learn how to use the Windows Explorer to view a disk's contents.

# VIEWING DRIVES, FOLDERS, AND FILES WITH THE WINDOWS EXPLORER

*In this lesson, you will learn how to use the Windows Explorer to view a disk's contents.*

## STARTING THE WINDOWS EXPLORER

To start the Windows Explorer, follow these steps:

1. Open the Start menu and choose Programs.

2. From the Programs menu, choose Windows Explorer. The Windows Explorer window appears (see Figure 11.1).

**Managing Files** The Windows Explorer in Windows 95 replaces Windows 3.1's File Manager.

## USING THE WINDOWS EXPLORER WINDOW

Figure 11.1 shows the Windows Explorer window. The All Folders window (the left side of the screen) shows all the folders on the selected drive (in this case, drive C).

Drive icons    All Folders window

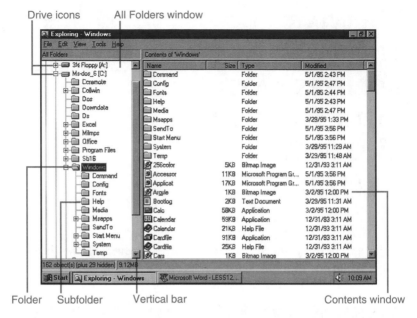

Folder    Subfolder    Vertical bar    Contents window

**FIGURE 11.1**    The Windows Explorer window, displaying the All Folders window.

The left side of the Windows Explorer window contains the folder list, a graphical representation of the folders and subfolders on your system. (The folder list on your screen will probably contain different folders from those shown in Figure 11.1.) In Figure 11.1, you can see that drive C contains a folder named *Windows*, and the Windows folder has many subfolders, including one named *Command*.

**Folders and Subfolders**    The folder that leads to all other folders (much like the trunk of a tree leads to all branches and leaves) is the *main folder*. In Figure 11.1 the main folder is C:\. Any folder can have a subfolder. *Subfolders* are like file folders within file folders; they help you organize your files. In Figure 11.1, Command is a subfolder of Windows.

The right side of the window contains a list of the files in the folder that's currently highlighted in the folder list. Notice that the folder icon next to the Windows folder (the highlighted folder) appears as an open folder. In this figure, the files in the Windows folder are listed in the right half of the Windows Explorer window.

## SELECTING FOLDERS

When you select a folder using the folders list, its contents are displayed on the right side of the Explorer window. To select a folder with the mouse, simply click on the folder you want. Table 11.1 shows the keys you can use to select a folder with the keyboard.

TABLE 11.1   KEYS FOR SELECTING A FOLDER

| KEY | FUNCTION |
| --- | --- |
| ↑ | Selects the folder above the selected one. |
| ↓ | Selects the folder below the selected one. |
| ← | Closes the selected folder. |
| → | Opens the selected folder. |
| Home | Selects the first folder in the folder list. |
| End | Selects the last folder in the folder list. |
| *First letter of folder name* | Selects the first folder that begins with that letter. Press the letter again if necessary, until you select the folder you want. |

## OPENING AND CLOSING FOLDERS

In Figure 11.1, the folders list shows the subfolders of the Windows folder. You can *close* (decrease the detail of) the folders list so that subfolders do not appear, or you can *open* (increase the detail of) the folders list so that folders many levels deep will all show. A plus sign (+) next to a folder indicates that there are subfolders to display; a minus sign (–) next to a folder indicates that the folder has been opened and can be closed.

To open or close a folder with the mouse, just double-click on the folder icon. To open or close a folder with the keyboard, use the arrow keys to select the folder and press + (plus) to open it or – (minus) to close it.

 **It's Only for Show**   Closing and opening affects this display only; it doesn't alter your folders in any way.

## CHANGING DRIVES

You can change drives to see the folders and files contained on a different disk. To change drives with the mouse, click on the drive icon at the top of the folders list. Using the keyboard, press the first number for the drive type (for example, press **3** for a 3.5" floppy drive). To change to drive C, use the arrow keys to highlight (C:).

# CHANGING THE WINDOWS EXPLORER DISPLAY

The commands in Windows Explorer's View menu enable you to change how the folders window and the files list window display information. You can control the size of the windows, whether or not the toolbar and status bar are displayed, and how the files in the files list window are displayed.

When you change the Windows Explorer's display settings to suit your needs, Windows remembers those settings. They remain the same every time you start Windows (until you change them again).

## SIZING THE WINDOWS

In the Windows Explorer screens you've seen so far, both the folders window and the list of files were shown. You can change the way each is shown by changing the amount of window space allotted to each. For example, you may want to see more files and less white space around the folders list. Follow these steps to change the way the window space is divided between the panes:

1. A vertical gray line appears in the Folders window, representing the divider between the two panes. Point to the gray line, and the mouse pointer changes to a short vertical bar with two arrows.

2. Drag the line to where you want it. The window display changes accordingly (see Figure 11.2).

Vertical bar has been moved to make files list larger.

**FIGURE 11.2**   The changed window.

**Changing the Display**  You change the size of the window panes in Windows 95's Explorer the same way you changed them in Windows 3.1's File Manager window.

## Changing the File List Display

By default, the Windows Explorer shows only the file names and icons for each folder. However, you can change the display to include more information about each file if you want. The View menu provides you with four options you can use to customize the file list display: Large Icons, Small Icons, List, and Details.

The View, List command tells Windows to display only the icons and file names for each folder (as shown in Figure 11.2). This is the default display.

Choose View, Details to have Windows display the following information about each file:

- Size in bytes
- File type (to describe the file—such as Folder, Application, Help, Settings, and so on)
- Last modification day and date

You can also change the size of the icons that Windows displays in the files list window. Choose View, Large Icons to display large icons with the file names beneath the icons. Choose View, Small Icons to display small icons with the file names to the right of the icons.

**Changing the Files List**   The View, Large Icons and View, Small Icons commands in Windows 95 are not available in Windows 3.1. The View, List and View, Details commands in Windows 95 replace the View, Partial Details and View, All Files Details commands in Windows 3.1.

## CONTROLLING THE ORDER OF THE DISPLAY

As you can see in Figure 11.2, the files in the folder are listed in alphabetical order by file name. If you prefer, you can have Windows arrange the icons by the following methods:

- Choose View, Arrange Icons, by Type to arrange files alphabetically by their file type.

- Choose View, Arrange Icons, by Size to arrange files from smallest to largest.

- Choose View, Arrange Icons, by Date to arrange files alphabetically by date from newest to oldest.

 **Controlling the Order of the Display**   The View, Arrange Icons command in Windows 95 replaces the View, Sort command in Windows 3.1.

## DISPLAYING THE TOOLBAR

You can display the Windows Explorer toolbar at the top of the Windows Explorer window (as shown in Figure 11.3) by choosing View, Toolbar. Then you can click on the buttons on the toolbar instead of choosing menu commands. Table 11.2 shows the buttons on the Windows Explorer toolbar.

Toolbar

Status bar

**Figure 11.3**    The Windows Explorer with the toolbar and status bar displayed.

**Table 11.2    Windows Explorer's Toolbar Buttons**

| Button | Name | Description |
|--------|------|-------------|
| | Up One Level | Displays the folder up one level from the folder currently displayed in the Folder text box. |
| | Cut | Cuts the selected file or folder and places it on the Clipboard. |
| | Copy | Copies the selected file or folder to the Clipboard. |
| | Paste | Pastes the contents of the Clipboard to the location selected in the list. |

| BUTTON | NAME | DESCRIPTION |
|--------|------|-------------|
| | Undo | Undoes last file or folder operation. |
| | Delete | Deletes the selected file or folder. |
| | Properties | Displays the properties of the selected file or folder. |
| | Large Icons | Displays large icons in the contents window. |
| | Small Icons | Displays small icons in the contents window. |
| | List | Displays a list of files and folders with names and icons. |
| | Details | Displays a detailed list of files and folders. |

## DISPLAYING THE STATUS BAR

Initially, Windows displays the status bar at the bottom of the Windows Explorer window (as shown in Figure 11.3). If you want to hide the status bar, open the View menu and select Status Bar (to deactivate it). To redisplay it, repeat the previous command sequence.

# CLOSING THE WINDOWS EXPLORER

If you're not going to use the Windows Explorer again right away, you should close it instead of minimizing it, to conserve system resources. To close the Windows Explorer, click the Close button or double-click the Control menu icon.

In this lesson, you learned how to use the Windows Explorer to examine the contents of a disk. In the next lesson, you'll learn how to create and delete files and folders.

# LESSON 12

# CREATING AND DELETING FILES AND FOLDERS

*In this lesson, you learn how to create and delete files and folders.*

## CREATING A FILE OR FOLDER

Some files and folders are created automatically when you install a program. For example, when you install Word for Windows, the installation program creates a folder on your hard drive and places the Word for Windows files in that folder. However, you can also create files and folders yourself.

There are several reasons you may want to create a folder. Many application installation programs create a folder when you install the application on your computer. If one of your application installation programs does not, you will want to create a folder for that application.

A more common reason to create a folder is to store document files. For example, you may want to create a folder to store documents you create with WordPad so the document files won't be scattered among the more than one hundred Windows program files in the Windows folder. Having a separate folder for WordPad documents makes it much easier to find and manipulate the documents you create.

## CREATING A FOLDER WITH WINDOWS EXPLORER

To create a folder using the Windows Explorer, follow these steps:

1. Open the Start menu and choose Programs.

2. From the Programs menu, choose Windows Explorer. The Windows Explorer window appears.

3. Highlight the folder in the folders window under which you want to create the new folder. (The folder you create will be a subfolder of the folder you highlight.) If you don't want the new folder to be a subfolder of another folder, highlight the (C:) folder.

4. Open the File menu and choose New. Then choose Folder. A folder icon named **New Folder** appears at the bottom of the files list.

5. Type the new folder name using up to 255 characters (including spaces) in the text box that appears next to the new folder icon. The name you type replaces the words **"New Folder"** as you type.

6. Press **Enter**, and Windows renames the new folder.

**Creating and Deleting Folders**   The File, New Folder command in Windows 95 replaces the File, Create Directory command in Windows 3.1. You use the same process to delete a folder in Windows 95 (see "Deleting a File or Folder") that you did to delete a directory in Windows 3.1.

## CREATING A FOLDER WITH MY COMPUTER

To create a folder with My Computer, follow these steps:

1. In My Computer, open the icon or folder in which you want to create a folder.

2. Open My Computer's File menu and select New. Windows creates a new folder icon.

3. Type a new name for the folder and press **Enter**.

# DELETING A FILE OR FOLDER

There will come a time when you need to delete a file or folder. For example, you may have created a file or folder by mistake, you may want to remove the files or folder for an application you no longer use, or you may need to make more room on your hard drive.

 **Better Safe Than Sorry** Before you delete anything, it is a good idea to make a backup copy of any files or folders you might need later. See Lesson 13 for directions on how to copy files and folders.

To delete a file or folder, follow these steps:

1. In a My Computer window or the Windows Explorer folders list, select the file or folder to delete. Be aware that when you delete a folder, Windows 95 deletes all files in that folder.

2. Choose File, Delete or press the **Delete** key. The Confirm Folder Delete dialog box appears, indicating what will be deleted and asking you to confirm the deletion.

3. Check the Confirm Folder Delete dialog box carefully to make certain you are deleting what you intended to delete.

4. Select Yes.

**Deleting a File or Folder**   The File, Delete commands in Windows 95 and Windows 3.1 are similar. In Windows 95, however, you see only the Confirm Delete dialog box; in Windows 3.1, you see the Delete dialog box and then the Confirm Delete dialog box. Also, Windows 95 deletes the files from the Windows Explorer or the My Computer window and moves them to the Recycle Bin. Then, from the Recycle Bin you can restore any files you might need.

**I Didn't Mean to Do That!**   If you delete a folder or file by mistake, immediately choose Edit, Undo Delete to restore the deleted folder(s) and file(s).

# WORKING WITH THE RECYCLE BIN

The files you delete in Windows are stored temporarily in the Recycle Bin. You can retrieve files from the Recycle Bin if you decide you need them again, or you can purge the deleted files when you're sure you no longer need them. By purging deleted files, you make more room on your disk.

To retrieve files you've deleted, follow these steps:

1. Double-click the Recycle Bin icon. The Recycle Bin window appears.

2. Click on the file you want to retrieve. To select multiple files, hold down **Ctrl** and click on each file.

3. Open the File menu and choose Restore. Windows restores the files to their original locations.

Follow these steps to purge deleted files in the Recycle Bin:

1. Open the File menu and select Empty Recycle Bin. A confirmation dialog box appears.

**2.** Choose Yes to delete all the files.

**3.** Click the Close button to close the Recycle Bin window.

 **Purge Files Individually**   To delete only one file from the Recycle Bin, select the file, open the File menu, choose Delete, and click on Yes. Windows purges that file only.

 **Recycle Bin**   The Recycle Bin is a new feature in Windows 95; it is not available in Windows 3.1.

In this lesson, you learned how to create and delete files and folders. In the next lesson, you'll learn how to move and copy files and folders.

# MOVING AND COPYING FILES AND FOLDERS

*In this lesson, you learn how to select multiple files and folders and how to copy and move them.*

## SELECTING MULTIPLE FILES OR FOLDERS

To really speed up operations, you will want to select multiple files or folders and then execute commands that affect the entire group. For example, you may want to select several files to copy to a disk. Copying them all at once is much faster than copying each file individually. The following sections explain how you can select multiple files and folders.

### SELECTING MULTIPLE CONTIGUOUS FILES OR FOLDERS

It is easy to select multiple files or folders that are displayed contiguously in Windows Explorer's files list window or My Computer.

**Contiguous Files** When the files that you want to select are listed next to each other in the Windows Explorer, without any files that you don't want in between them, they are *contiguous*.

To select contiguous files or folders with the mouse:

1.  Click the first file or folder that you want to select. When you click it, it becomes highlighted.

2.  Hold down the **Shift** key and click the last file or folder that you want to select. All the items between (and including) the first and last selections are highlighted. Figure 13.1 shows a selection of contiguous files.

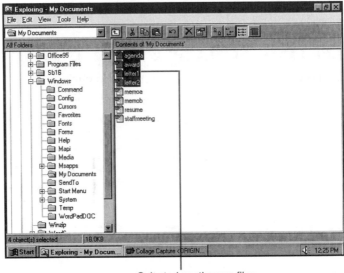

Selected contiguous files

**FIGURE 13.1**   Selected contiguous files are highlighted.

To select contiguous files or folders with the keyboard:

1.  Use the arrow keys to move the highlight to the first file or folder that you want to select. (Press **Tab** to move the highlight bar between the folders window and the files list window.)

2. Hold down the **Shift** key and use the arrow keys to extend the highlight to the last file or folder you want to select.

To deselect a contiguous group of files or folders, select a file or folder outside the selected items.

## SELECTING NONCONTIGUOUS FILES OR FOLDERS

Often, the files or folders you want to select are noncontiguous: they are separated by several files that you do not want. To select such noncontiguous files or folders, you use the Ctrl key.

To select items with the mouse, hold down the **Ctrl** key and click on the files or folders you want. Each item you click on becomes highlighted and remains highlighted until you release the Ctrl key. Figure 13.2 shows a selection of multiple noncontiguous files. To deselect items with the mouse, click on any file or folder.

**FIGURE 13.2**   Selecting multiple noncontiguous files.

**Narrowing the Selection** If you want to select or deselect files with related names, choose the Tools, Find, Files
or Folders command. Enter the characters you want to
find in the Named text box and choose (C:) from the Look
in drop-down list. Then choose Find Now. When Windows
95 displays the files you want to select or deselect,
choose Edit, Select, All in the menu bar of the Find dialog
box to select all the files in the Search Results window.
Then deselect the files you don't want selected. For example, you may want to select all WordPad document
files with a .DOC extension and then deselect a few of the
files individually if you don't want them all for your activity.
Lesson 14 explains how to use the Find command.

**Selecting Files or Folders** You select files or folders in
Windows 95 the same way you select files and directories
in Windows 3.1.

# Moving or Copying Files or Folders

To move or copy files or folders through the Windows Explorer or
My Computer, you *drag and drop*—that is, you select the items you
want from your *source* folder, "drag" them to the *destination*
folder, and "drop" them there. You'll learn the details of using
this technique later in this section.

**Move vs. Copy** When you *move* the file or folder, it no
longer exists in its original location, but only in the new
location. When you *copy* a file or folder, the original file or
folder remains in its original location, and a copy of the file
or folder is placed in a second location.

Before you move or copy, make sure the source file or folder is visible, so you can highlight the file(s) you're going to drag. Also, make sure that the destination drive or folder is visible. In Figure 13.3, My Documents (the source folder), the Memoa file (the *source* file), and the empty WordPadDOC folder (the *destination* folder) are all visible.

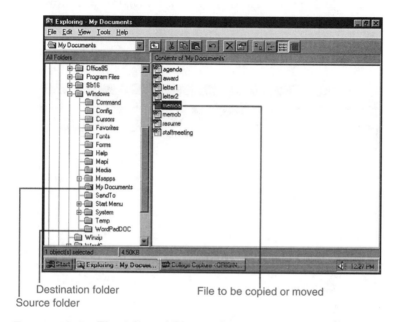

Destination folder          File to be copied or moved
Source folder

**FIGURE 13.3**   The selected file can be moved or copied.

## COPYING FILES AND FOLDERS

With the mouse, use this procedure to copy:

1. Select the files or folders to copy.

2. Press the **Ctrl** key and drag the files or folders to the destination drive or folder.

3. Release the mouse button and the Ctrl key.

With the keyboard, use this procedure to copy:

1. Select the files or folders to copy.

2. Open the Edit menu and choose Copy.

3. Select the destination drive or folder.

4. Open the Edit menu and choose Paste. Figure 13.4 shows the result of the copy and paste operations. The WordPad document file has been copied into the WordPadDOC folder.

**FIGURE 13.4** The completed copy operation.

 **The File Is Already There** If you attempt to copy a file or folder to a location in which a file or folder with the exact same name exists, Windows 95 lets you know with a message that says **This folder already contains a file called 'filename'. Would you like to replace the existing file with this one?** Choose Yes to replace the existing file or No to stop the copy operation.

## MOVING FILES AND FOLDERS

With the mouse, follow these steps to complete a move:

1. Select the files or folders to move.

2. Drag the files or folders to the destination drive or folder.

3. Release the mouse button.

With the keyboard, complete a move using these steps:

1. Select the files or folders to move.

2. Open the Edit menu and choose Cut.

3. Select the destination drive or folder.

4. Open the Edit menu and choose Paste.

**Copying and Moving Files and Folders**   Copying and moving files and folders in Windows 95 and Windows 3.1 are similar. The Edit, Copy and Edit, Cut commands in Windows 95 replace the File, Copy and File, Move commands in Windows 3.1. Also, the Copy and Move confirmation dialog boxes you saw in Windows 3.1 do not appear in Windows 95, which makes it quicker to copy and move files and folders.

**Wrong Move or Copy?**   If you move or copy the wrong files or folders, you can choose Edit, Undo Copy in the Windows Explorer menu bar or click the Undo button on the Windows Explorer toolbar to undo the operation.

In this lesson, you learned how to select multiple files and folders and how to copy and move files and folders. In the next lesson, you'll learn how to rename and find files and folders.

# Renaming and Finding Files and Folders

*In this lesson, you learn how to rename and find files and folders.*

## Renaming Files or Folders

To rename your files, follow these steps:

1. In the Windows Explorer or a My Computer window, select the file or folder you want to rename.

2. Choose File, Rename. A box appears around the file or folder name, and the name is highlighted.

3. Type the new name for the file or folder. As you type, the new name replaces the old name. Press **Enter** when you finish typing.

 **It Worked Yesterday**   Never rename program files. Many applications will not work if their files have been renamed.

 **Renaming Files or Folders**   The File, Rename commands in Windows 95 and Windows 3.1 are similar. However, you type the new name next to the icon in Windows 95, whereas in Windows 3.1, you type the new name into the Rename dialog box.

# SEARCHING FOR A FILE

As you create more files, the ability to find a specific file becomes more critical. You can search for either a single file or a group of files with similar names using the Tools Find command. To search for a group of files, use the asterisk wild card (*) with a partial file name to narrow the search. You can also perform a partial name search without wild cards, search by last modification date, save complex searches, and do a full text search. Table 14.1 shows some search examples and their potential results.

 **Wild Cards**   When you're not sure of the file name you want to find, you can use the asterisk wild card (*) to replace multiple characters in the file name or the question mark wild card (?) to replace one character in the file name.

TABLE 14.1   SEARCH EXAMPLES AND THEIR RESULTS

| CHARACTERS ENTERED FOR SEARCH | SAMPLE SEARCH RESULTS |
| --- | --- |
| mem?.doc | mem1.doc, mem2.doc, mem5.doc |
| mem1.doc | mem1.doc |
| mem*.doc | mem1.doc, mem2.doc, mem11.doc |
| c*.exe | calc.exe, calendar.exe |
| *.exe | calc.exe, calendar.exe, notepad.exe |
| c*.* | calc.exe, calendar.exe, class.doc |

To search for a file, follow these steps:

1. From the Windows Explorer, click the Start menu, select Find, and select Files or Folders. The Find dialog box appears (see Figure 14.1).

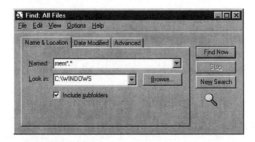

FIGURE 14.1   The completed Find dialog box.

2. In the Named text box, enter the characters you want to find, using wild cards to identify unknown characters.

3. If you want to search the entire drive, choose **Ms-dos_6 (C:)** in the Look In text box (if it's not already there) and make sure the Include subfolders check box is selected.

   If you want to search only the main folder, make sure the Include Subfolders check box is not selected.

   If you want to search a specific folder, click the Browse button and select a folder from the folders list.

4. If you want to search for a file according to its last modification date, select the Date Modified tab and select the date options you want.

5. If you want to search for a certain type of file, select the Advanced tab and choose a file type in the Of Type drop-down list box.

6. Select the Find Now button to begin the search. The search results window appears under the Find dialog box, showing the files that were found (see Figure 14.2).

FIGURE 14.2   The search results.

**Bypass the Windows Explorer to Find a File**   You can also search for a file using the Find command in the Start menu. To quickly find a file, click the Start button and choose Find, Files or Folders instead of starting the Windows Explorer and using the Tools, Find, Files or Folders command.

**Searching for a File**   The Find command in Windows 95 replaces the File, Search command in Windows 3.1.

In this lesson, you learned how to rename a file or folder and search for a file or folder. In the next lesson, you'll learn how to work with fonts in Windows.

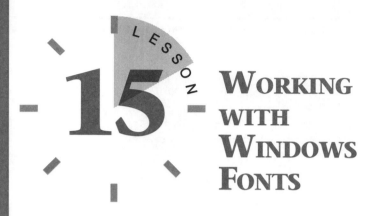

# WORKING WITH WINDOWS FONTS

*In this lesson, you learn to find what fonts you have, display font samples, add new fonts, and delete fonts.*

## FINDING OUT WHAT FONTS YOU HAVE

Many printers can print more than one character style or typeface (called a *font*). Check your printer manual to see if your printer is capable of printing multiple fonts. If it is, you will want to check the font setup in Windows 95 before you print. Fonts may be stored on floppy disks or on cartridges that slide into the printer.

Windows provides and supports different fonts, including TrueType fonts. Bit-mapped fonts store a unique bit map (or graphic) image for each font in each size. TrueType fonts are easily accessible, built-in, scalable fonts that don't care what kind of printer or display monitor you have.

When you set up Windows 95, the fonts for your printer were identified. Figure 15.1 shows the list of fonts in the Properties sheet for an HP DeskJet 500 printer. Font cartridges are available for this printer, and the Cartridge **B: Prestige Elite** is selected. You can select a maximum of two cartridges for this printer at any time.

Use the Fonts page in the Properties sheet (shown in Figure 15.1) to see the Font options. From this dialog box, you can determine which font cartridges are installed.

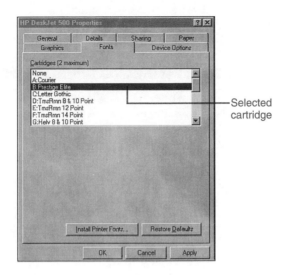

Selected cartridge

**FIGURE 15.1**   Selecting a font cartridge.

To check the font cartridge setup:

1. From the Start menu, choose Settings, Printers. The Printers window appears.

2. From the Printers window, right-click the printer icon. The shortcut menu appears.

3. Choose Properties. The Properties sheet appears.

4. Click the Fonts tab. The font options for the selected printer appear (see Figure 15.1).

5. If your fonts are stored on cartridges, highlight the cartridge(s) you'll use (based on the maximum number identified in the dialog box).

Use the Fonts folder shown in Figure 15.2 to check the setup of the fonts stored on the hard disk drive. Follow these steps:

1. From the Start menu, choose Settings. The Settings menu appears.

2. Choose Control Panel. The Control Panel window appears.

3. Choose Fonts. The Fonts window appears (see Figure 15.2).

TrueType
font icon

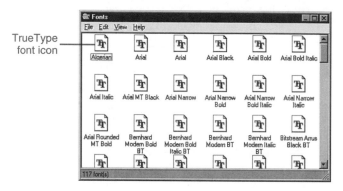

**Figure 15.2**   The Fonts folder.

# Displaying Font Samples

Windows displays detailed information about any font you select in the Fonts window. You can see a sample of a font and all the sizes it comes in on-screen, as well as print a copy of the sample font.

To display a font sample:

1. From the Start menu, choose Settings. The Settings menu appears.

2. Choose Control Panel. The Control Panel window appears.

3. Choose Fonts. The Fonts window appears.

4. Double-click a font and Windows displays a sample with all the sizes it comes in (see Figure 15.3).

5. Click the Print button in the font's dialog box to print font information and font size samples.

**FIGURE 15.3**   A font sample with all its sizes.

# INSTALLING FONTS FROM DISK

You may find that you want to add fonts to the operating environment. These fonts become available for use in all Windows applications. When you add a font to Windows, you use disk space (however, TrueType fonts take up much less space than bit-mapped fonts.)

To install fonts from disk, follow these steps:

1. From the Start menu, choose Settings. The Settings menu appears.

2. Choose Control Panel. The Control Panel window appears.

3. Choose Fonts. The Fonts window appears.

4. From the Fonts menu bar, choose File, Install New Font. The Add Fonts dialog box appears.

5. Insert the disk that contains the fonts you want to add into the correct drive.

6. In the Add Fonts dialog box, select the drive letter for the fonts disk (A:, B:, or D:) and click the OK button. The fonts available on the disk or CD appear in the List of Fonts list box.

7. Select the fonts you want to add and click the OK button. The fonts are copied to the Fonts folder.

## DELETING A FONT FROM DISK

Fonts take up space in active memory as well as on your hard disk. There may come a time when you want to either delete fonts you don't use from active memory, or remove them entirely from your disk. To delete a font, follow these steps:

1. From the Start menu, choose Settings. The Settings menu appears.

2. Choose Control Panel. The Control Panel window appears.

3. Choose Fonts. The Fonts window appears.

4. Select the fonts you want to delete.

5. From the Fonts menu bar, choose File, Delete. Windows asks you to confirm deleting the font(s).

6. Click the OK button. Windows removes the font(s) from disk.

 **Quickly delete the fonts**   You can drag the unwanted fonts to the Recycle Bin to quickly delete the fonts you no longer use.

In this lesson, you learned how to view, install, and delete fonts. In the next lesson, you'll learn how to set up Windows for printing.

# GETTING READY TO PRINT

*In this lesson, you learn to check printer installation and add a printer.*

## CHECKING THE PRINTER INSTALLATION

When you installed Windows 95, Setup configured any printers connected to your computer and created the links to those printers automatically. Before you attempt to print, however, you need to make sure the settings are correct.

To check the print setup from Windows 95, go to the Printers folder using the following steps:

1. From the Start menu, choose Settings. The Settings menu appears.

2. From the Settings menu, choose Printers. The Printers folder appears (see Figure 16.1).

Double-click to add printers

Installed printers

**FIGURE 16.1** The Printers folder.

**TIP**

**Easy access to the Printers Folder** You can access the Printers folder from three other places in Windows 95: the My Computer window, the bottom of the folders list in the Windows Explorer, and the Control Panel Printers icon.

From the Printers folder, you can select the installed printer you want to check and open the Properties sheet to check the settings. To do so, right-click the printer icon in the Printers window to open the shortcut menu, then choose Properties to display the Properties sheet. Figure 16.2 shows the Properties sheet for the HP DeskJet 500 printer.

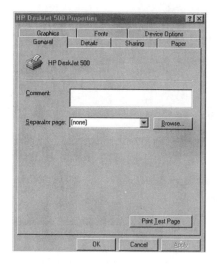

**FIGURE 16.2** The Properties sheet for the HP DeskJet 500 printer.

You can choose from the following tabs in the Properties sheet to check the settings.

• The General options include the printer name, comments, separator page, and print test page.

- The Details tab displays the details about your installed printer. On it, you see the port connection to which your printer is attached (Print to the following port). This port is usually LPT1 (for parallel printers) or COM1 (for serial printers).

 **Printer Port**   The connection on your computer to which your printer's cable is attached. If the port description indicates **Not Present**, Windows 95 doesn't detect that port on your computer. Check your printer manual to see whether your printer uses the parallel or serial port.

- The Paper options enable you to enter information about the paper size and paper source, and to set the orientation to either Portrait (the short side of the paper is at the top) or Landscape (the long side of the paper is at the top).

- The Graphics options enable you to enter information about resolution in dots per inch (the more dots the finer the resolution), dithering (none, coarse, fine, line art, error diffusion), and intensity (from darkest to lightest).

- The Fonts options list the installed printer fonts and enable you to install and remove printer fonts (see Lesson 15).

- The Device Options enable you to change the print quality and printer memory. Check your printer manual if you are not sure of the amount of memory in your printer.

 **Checking the Printer Installation**   The Printers folder in Windows 95 replaces the Printers feature in the Control Panel of Windows 3.1.

Once you have all the options set the way you want them, click the OK button in the Properties sheet to return to the Printers folder.

## SETTING A DEFAULT PRINTER

The *default printer* is the printer that the computer assumes is connected to your computer unless you select another printer. The default printer is the first one that appears in the Printers folder list. Windows automatically sets up a default printer when you install Windows. Almost all Windows 95 applications print using the Printers folder and the default printer defined through it. To set up a default printer:

1. From the Printers folder, double-click the icon that represents the printer you want to set as the default. The print queue window opens.

2. In the print queue, choose the Printer, Set as Default command to specify the default printer.

**Quick Method** Right-click on a printer icon and choose Set As Default from the shortcut menu.

## CHECKING YOUR EQUIPMENT

In addition to making sure Windows 95 is ready for printing, you'll want to check your equipment. Be sure to double-check the following things:

- Is the cable between the computer and the printer securely attached on each end?
- Is the printer turned on?
- Is the printer ready for the computer's transmission with the On Line light on?
- Is paper loaded in the printer?

## ADDING A PRINTER

The Add Printer wizard in the Printers folder lets you add new printers to the list of installed printers available in the Printers folder. This wizard simplifies the process of adding a printer.

To add a new printer, follow these steps:

1. In the Printers window, double-click the Add Printer icon. The Add Printer Wizard dialog box appears.

2. Click the Next button.

3. If you are using a network, choose Local Printer or Network Printer and click the Next button.

4. Select a printer from the Manufacturers list box. The wizard displays a list of printer models in the Models list box.

5. Select a printer model.

6. Choose OK, then follow the prompts in each wizard dialog box to install the new printer.

**What Disk?**   When you install new features to your Windows environment, have your installation diskettes close at hand. In the example above, Windows will probably ask you to insert one of the disks containing the printer drivers before it can carry out your instructions.

**Adding a Printer**   You can add a printer with the Add Printer Wizard in Windows 95 instead of choosing the Add button in the Printer dialog box in Windows 3.1.

In this lesson, you learned how to check your printer's installation and add a printer. In the next lesson, you learn how to manage print jobs in Windows.

# PRINTING WITH THE PRINTERS FOLDER

*In this lesson, you learn to manage jobs you send to any printer.*

## PRINTING FROM A WINDOWS APPLICATION

To print from any Windows application, choose File, Print. A Print dialog box appears for you to specify a number of options. The options available depend on the application. When you click OK in this dialog box, the application hands off the font and file information to the Printers folder. This enables you to continue working in your application while your job is printing. The Printers folder acts as the "middleman" between your printer and the application from which you are printing.

**Print Jobs** Windows creates a print job (or simply a job) when you choose the Print command from the application you are working in.

**Printers Folder** Each printer icon in the Printers folder in Windows 95 handles print jobs rather than using a separate Print Manager in Windows 3.1.

# CHECKING THE PRINT QUEUE

When you print a document, the printer usually begins processing the job immediately. But what happens if the printer is working on another job that you (or someone else if you're working on
a network printer) sent? In this case, the Printers folder acts as a
print queue and holds the job until the printer is ready for it.

**Print Queue**  A holding area for jobs waiting to be
printed. If you were to list the contents of the queue, the
jobs would appear in the order they were sent to the
Printer.

Figure 17.1 shows a document in the print queue. As you can see,
the print queue window displays the document name, status,
owner, progress (pages), and started at (time and date). Notice also
that the printer's status shows that it is printing. This indicates
the document was just sent to the queue and is beginning to
print.

| Document Name | Status | Owner | Progress | Started At |
|---|---|---|---|---|
| Microsoft Word - EW7-03.DOC | Printing | | 1 of 16 pages | 4:19:39 PM 6/22/95 |
| Microsoft Word - EW7-01.DOC | | | 18 page(s) | 4:19:51 PM 6/22/95 |
| Microsoft Word - EW7-02.DOC | | | 25 page(s) | 4:20:00 PM 6/22/95 |

HP DeskJet 500
Printer  Document  View  Help
3 jobs in queue

**FIGURE 17.1**   The print queue window.

To display the print queue, follow these steps:

1. Click the Start button, and choose Settings. The Settings
   menu appears.

2. Choose Printers and the Printers folder appears.

3. Double-click the printer icon for the printer to which you are printing. The print queue window appears with a list of *queued* documents. If no documents are waiting to print, there won't be any jobs listed below the column headings.

 **Display the print queue quickly**   Double-click the printer icon that appears on the taskbar immediately after printing a document.

# Controlling the Print Job

You can control print jobs once they're in the queue. This includes changing the order in which the jobs print, pausing and resuming the print job, and deleting a job before it prints.

## Reordering Jobs in the Queue

To change the order of a job in the queue, simply drag the job entry to a new position in the list.

 **First Come, First Served**   You can't reorder or place a job before the job that is currently printing.

## Pausing and Resuming the Print Queue

You may want to pause the queue and then resume printing later. For example, the paper in the printer may be misaligned. Pausing the print queue will give you time to correct the problem.

To pause the print queue, choose Printer, Pause Printing or press **Alt+P** and **A** while in the print queue window. To resume printing, choose Printer, Pause Printing again from the print queue menu bar or press **Alt+P** and **A**.

**Printer Stalled**   Your printer may stall while it's processing your print job. If it does, Windows displays the word **stalled** in the printer status line. Press **Alt+P** and **A** to start printing again. This gets the printer going again, but chances are that a problem such as the printer being out of paper or ink caused the printer to stall. If so, the queue will stall again, and you'll have to refer to your printer manual or contact a technical person to help you.

## DELETING A PRINT JOB

Sometimes, you'll send a document to be printed and then change your mind. For example, you may think of other text to add to the document or realize you forgot to spell-check your work. In such a case, deleting the print job is easy. Follow these steps:

1. Click the Start button, and choose Settings. The Settings menu appears.

2. Choose Printers. The Printers folder appears.

3. Double-click the printer icon for the printer to which you are printing. The print queue window appears.

4. Select the job to delete.

5. Choose Document, Cancel Printing.

 **Clear the Queue!**   To delete all the files in the print queue, choose Printer, Purge Print Jobs from the print queue menu bar or click the Close button in the top right corner of the window.

In this lesson, you learned how to control print jobs. In the next lesson, you learn how to change the desktop and regional settings.

# 18 CONTROLLING THE APPEARANCE OF WINDOWS 95

*In this lesson, you'll learn to control specific aspects of the Control Panel, such as on-screen colors, what appears on your desktop, and the locale and units settings.*

## CHANGING YOUR DESKTOP

The Control Panel is a folder available through the Settings menu that enables you to control various aspects of Windows 95 (see Figure 18.1).

The Display Properties sheet lets you control many things about your desktop. To access this dialog box, follow these steps:

**FIGURE 18.1** The Windows 95 Control Panel.

1. From the Start menu, choose Settings, Control Panel. The Control Panel appears (see Figure 18.1).

 2. Double-click the Display icon. The Display Properties dialog box appears.

 **Display Settings**   The Display icon in Windows 95's Control Panel replaces the Color and Desktop icons in Windows 3.1's Control Panel.

The Display Properties sheet contains several tabs that control different sets of options. The following sections explain how to use these tabs.

## CHANGING THE DESKTOP BACKGROUND

You can change a number of visual and performance elements of your desktop through the Control Panel. To change the desktop background, follow these steps:

1. Open the Display Properties sheet (as described earlier in the lesson).

2. If necessary, click the Background tab. The Pattern and Wallpaper options appear in the window.

3. Select the options you want, and choose OK. Figure 18.2 shows the Rivets wallpaper and Tile display options selected in the window. Tile displays wallpaper on the entire desktop and Center displays wallpaper only in the center of the desktop.

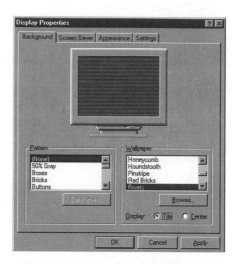

FIGURE 18.2    Rivets is selected in the wallpaper options.

From the Background page, you can change any of the following options:

**Pattern**    Select the pattern to be displayed on the desktop. You can choose from a number of simple, two-color patterns; see the sample screen displayed at the top of the dialog box to see an example.

**Wallpaper**    More elaborate than the Pattern selection, the Wallpaper option enables you to display .BMP files on your desktop. Windows 95 comes with some very attractive wallpapers. The wallpaper you select is displayed in the sample screen at the top of the dialog box.

**Display**    Select the type of display you want for the wallpaper. Tiled wallpaper repeats pictures to cover the whole desktop. Centered wallpaper places one picture in the middle of the desktop; extra space around the wallpaper is filled with the desktop color.

## SETTING A SCREEN SAVER

Even though screen savers are no longer needed to prevent damage to your monitor, they're still fun to use anyway. If you select a screen saver, Windows automatically blanks the screen and runs a pattern across it anytime your computer is inactive for the default length of time. To return to the screen you left and continue working, press a key or move the mouse.

To select a screen saver, follow these steps:

1. Open the Display Properties sheet (as described earlier in this lesson).

2. Click the Screen Saver tab.

3. Select a screen saver from the Screen Saver drop-down list box by clicking on the down arrow (↓). The screen saver options appear.

4. Click on a screen saver option in the list. The sample screen at the top of the page shows the current selection.

5. In the Wait text box, enter the number of minutes you want to delay the screen saver, and then choose OK.

## CHANGING APPEARANCE SETTINGS

With the Control Panel, you can change the appearance of your desktop by setting the colors of many components in Windows 95. The capability to control the color of certain Windows elements can help you learn to use the program faster: you're able to look for a particular color and shape, instead of just a shape. Or you can adjust the colors displayed on your color monitor just for a change of pace.

Follow these steps to change the Windows screen colors from the Control Panel:

1. Open the Display Properties sheet (as described earlier in the lesson).

2. Click the Appearance tab. The color scheme options appear in the window.

3. Select a color scheme from the Scheme drop-down list box by clicking the down arrow or by pressing **Alt+S** and then **Alt+O**. The predefined scheme options appear.

4. Use the arrow keys to scroll through the scheme options. The display above the Scheme text box illustrates the current selection. Select the scheme you want to use.

5. Press **Enter** to make your choice. Figure 18.3 shows the Slate color scheme selected in the Appearance page.

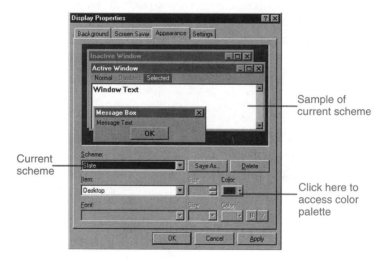

**FIGURE 18.3**    The Slate scheme as selected on the Appearance page.

After you become more comfortable with Windows 95, go into the Appearance page and create your own color scheme. You can assign different colors to the various Windows elements (title bar, buttons, menus, and so on). To do so, click on the element in the sample area that you want to change, and choose a color from the Color drop-down list. To save your creation as a Windows 95 scheme, click the Save As button, enter a name for the color scheme, and choose OK.

---

 **Color Scheme**   A color scheme is a set of predefined or customized colors that applies a different color to a different part of the screen. Color schemes make each Windows element easy to identify.

---

# Changing Regional Settings

Most readers will use Windows 95 in the United States. However, if you work in an international setting, you may want to make some changes in the Regional Settings Properties sheet. You can configure Windows to use settings familiar to your region, nationality, and number system. For example, if a United States firm creates letters or documents to be sent abroad to Spain, regional settings would benefit everyone by ensuring that all numeric and other settings are indigenous to Spain. Follow these steps to control the regional settings:

1. From the Start menu, choose Settings, Control Panel. The Control Panel window opens.

2. Double-click the Regional Settings icon. The Regional Settings Properties sheet appears (see Figure 18.4).

3. Make the selections for the changes you desire.

4. Choose OK and the changes are made.

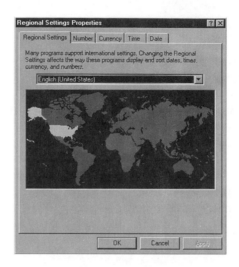

FIGURE 18.4    The Regional Settings Properties sheet.

In the Regional Settings Properties sheet, you can make changes on any of the following pages:

- **Regional Settings**    Windows has a number of standard locale settings on how units are displayed, page setup defaults, and so on. Use the Locale option on the Regional Settings page to choose the locale setting you want to use.

- **Number**    Use the Number options to change the way Windows displays numbers.

- **Currency**    Use the Currency options to change the way Windows displays positive and negative currency values.

- **Time**    Use the Time options to change the way Windows displays time values.

- **Date**    Use the Date options to change the way Windows displays long and short dates.

**Regional Settings**  The Regional Settings icon in Windows 95's Control Panel replaces the International Settings icon in Windows 3.1's Control Panel.

In this lesson, you learned to change the desktop and change regional settings from the Control Panel. In the next lesson, you'll learn how to change hardware settings from the Control Panel.

## LESSON 19
# CONTROLLING HARDWARE SETTINGS

*In this lesson, you learn to alter the date and time, modify mouse, keyboard, and multimedia settings, and add new hardware.*

## ALTERING THE DATE AND TIME

You use the Control Panel to set your computer's system date and time, which is used to time-stamp files as you create or modify them. The time appears on the right side of the Windows 95 taskbar. Also, many applications allow you to automatically insert the date and time on-screen or when you print. Always make sure the date and time are correct.

**Hardware Settings** The Mouse, Keyboard, and Date/Time icons in Windows 95's Control Panel are the same as those in Windows 3.1. The MultiMedia, Sounds, and Add New Hardware icons in Windows 95's Control Panel replace the Sound and Drivers icons in Windows 3.1's Control Panel.

To check or set the date and time, follow these steps:

1. From the Start menu, choose Settings, Control Panel. The Control Panel opens.

2. Double-click the Date/Time icon. The Date/Time Properties sheet appears (see Figure 19.1).

> **Setting the Date/Time** Double-click on the time that
> **TIP** appears on the far right side in the taskbar to display the
> Date/Time Properties sheet.

3. Press the **Tab** key or use the mouse to move between sections in the Date and Time boxes.

4. To change the date using the mouse, click the drop down arrow next to the month and click on a month in the list. To change the year, click the up or down arrow to increase or decrease the year value. To change the day, click on a number in the calendar month display.

5. To change the time, double-click on the portion of the time you want to change and click the up or down arrow button to increase or decrease the value accordingly.

6. Select OK or press **Enter** to accept the changes you have made. Select Cancel or press **Esc** to close the dialog box without saving changes.

 **Time Zone**   Using settings on the Time Zone tab in Windows 95, you can change the time zone that you work in. If you live in a time zone where daylight savings time changes, choose the Automatically Adjust clock for daylight saving changes options on the Time Zone page. Windows automatically adjusts your computer's clock when daylight saving time changes. The Time Zone feature isn't available in Windows 3.1.

FIGURE 19.1   The Date/Time Properties sheet.

**Date and Time Incorrect?** If the date and time are still incorrect the next time you start Windows, your computer's clock battery may be dead.

# MODIFYING MOUSE SETTINGS

By double-clicking the Mouse icon in the Control Panel, you can access a dialog box in which you can modify the following settings for your mouse:

**Buttons** The Right-handed button configuration option makes the left button the Normal Select/Normal Drag button, and the right button the Context Menu/Special Drag button. The Left-handed button configuration option makes the right button the Context Menu/Special Drag button, and the left button the Normal Select/Normal Drag button. The Double-Click Speed option controls the amount of time allowed between the first and second click so your action is recognized as a double-click and not just two single clicks.

**Pointers** The Scheme option changes the size and shape of the mouse pointer.

**Motion** With the Pointer Trail option, you can turn on or off a trail of mouse pointers that follow the pointer movement. The Pointer Speed sets the speed of mouse tracking (how fast/far the pointer moves when you move the mouse).

**General** The Name option enables you to specify the mouse driver. If the mouse driver doesn't appear in the Name list box, you can install the mouse driver you want to use by clicking the Change button. Windows prompts you to insert the disk that contains the mouse driver you want to install. Follow the prompts to install the mouse driver.

 **Try it, You'll Like It** As a precaution, always use the Test area to try new settings before you leave the screen. For example, you may need to test the double-click speed; if you set it all the way to Fast, you may not be able to double-click fast enough for it to register.

To modify these settings, follow these steps:

1. From the Control Panel, double-click the Mouse icon. The Mouse Properties sheet appears.

2. Enter the settings as desired, then test them in the Test area.

3. Select OK or press **Enter** to accept the changes you have made. Select Cancel or press **Esc** to close without saving changes.

## CHANGING KEYBOARD SETTINGS

With the keyboard settings, you can change how long you have to hold a key down before the character starts repeating. Follow these steps to change the response of the keyboard:

1. From the Control Panel, double-click the Keyboard icon. The Keyboard Properties sheet appears.

2. Enter the settings as desired. Then, you can test the repeat rate in the Test area below the Repeat Rate option.

3. Select OK or press **Enter** to accept the changes you have made. Select Cancel or press **Esc** to close without saving changes.

## CHANGING MULTIMEDIA SETTINGS

Multimedia is for changing audio, video, and MIDI settings. Normally, these Multimedia settings should not be changed. Windows sets up these options automatically during installation for optimum use.

To affect sound, follow these steps:

1. From the Control Panel, double-click the Multimedia icon. The Multimedia Properties sheet appears.

2. To change audio settings, click the Audio tab. If you don't have a sound card in your computer, the Preferred Device selections are grayed out (unavailable).

3. If you have a sound card, you can select a Preferred Device for Playback and Recording. You can also select the volume you want for Playback and Recording.

4. To change video settings, click the Video tab. It's recommended that you run video clips at their original size. Otherwise, the video may appear grainy if you change the window size or choose the Full Screen option.

5. To change MIDI settings, click the MIDI tab. You can change the instrument (generally used by games) on which Windows plays the MIDI output, create your own custom MIDI output configuration, and add a new instrument.

6. To change CD Music settings, click the CD Music tab. If you have more than one CD-ROM drive, you can specify which drive you want the Media Player, CD Player, and other programs to use as the default drive. You also can change the volume for your CD Player's headphones.

7. To change advanced multimedia settings, click the Advanced tab. You see a list of multimedia device categories. Double-click a category to see a list of multimedia devices. To change the specific settings for a device, right-click a device and choose Properties. Then make the necessary changes to the settings for the device.

8. Select OK or press **Enter** to accept the changes you have made. Select Cancel or press **Esc** to close without saving changes.

# CHANGING SOUNDS SETTINGS

The Sounds applet in the Control Panel lets you assign individual sounds to events. Controlling multimedia responses associated with actions or events can be simple or complex. At the simplest level, you can control the warning beep when you make an error or perform an action Windows doesn't recognize.

If you have a sound card in your computer, you can set sounds for a variety of events. Without a sound card all you hear is a beep.

To change sounds settings:

1. From the Control Panel, double-click the Sounds icon. The Sounds Properties sheet appears.

2. Select the different Events and assign a Name sound for each one. Click the icon in the Preview box and then click the Play button (the button with a right arrow) to the right of the Preview box to test your sound selection.

3. Select OK or press **Enter** to accept the changes you have made. Select Cancel or press **Esc** to close without saving changes.

# ADDING NEW HARDWARE

If you want to add a new piece of hardware to your computer, you can use the New Hardware wizard to install the new hardware. For example, you may want to install a new video card, disk device, or mouse. To add a video display adapter driver, use the Display Properties sheet and choose the Settings tab. You can add a printer by using the Printers folder and the Add Printer wizard. External devices such as modems are best installed by using their own installation wizard such as the Install Modem wizard.

To add new hardware, follow these steps:

1. From the Control Panel select the Add New Hardware icon. The Add New Hardware Wizard dialog box appears.

2. Follow the instructions in each wizard dialog box to install the desired device.

In this lesson, you learned how to set the system date and time, adjust mouse and keyboard settings, and install new hardware. In the next lesson, you learn how to create shortcuts, rearrange your Start menu, and use property sheets.

# CUSTOMIZING THE DESKTOP

*In this lesson, you learn to create shortcuts, rearrange commands on the Start menu, and change options in the property dialog boxes.*

## CREATING SHORTCUTS

You can create a shortcut that takes you to any object in the Windows 95 user interface. Then, you can place that object anywhere else in the user interface or in an application. For example, you can create a shortcut to a file, program, network folder, Control Panel tool, or disk drive. The shortcut is represented by an icon with a small arrow in the lower left corner (see Figure 20.1). The arrow is called a "shortcut" arrow and indicates that you can use this icon as a shortcut to an object.

When you double-click the shortcut icon, the object to which the shortcut is pointing is opened. For example, you can create a shortcut to Microsoft Word by placing a Microsoft Word shortcut icon on the desktop. Then, when you click on the shortcut icon, Windows 95 opens Microsoft Word.

FIGURE 20.1   Windows 95 shortcut icon for Microsoft Word.

You can create a shortcut for any object by right-clicking on the object and choosing Create Shortcut. The instructions below explain how to create a shortcut to a program folder:

1. Click the Start button and choose Programs, Windows Explorer. The Windows Explorer window appears.

2. Right-click the folder for which you want to create a shortcut. The shortcut menu appears.

3. Choose Create Shortcut. The shortcut icon appears.

4. Drag the shortcut icon from the window to any place on the desktop.

To delete a shortcut icon, click on the icon to select it, then press the **Delete** key. You are prompted to confirm the deletion. Choose Yes to delete the shortcut icon and it disappears.

 **More Shortcuts, Less Work** Windows 95 provides shortcuts that reduce the time and actions you have to perform to get your work done in the Windows 95 environment. These shortcuts aren't available in Windows 3.1.

## CUSTOMIZING THE START MENU

You can move frequently used commands in the Start menu to a more convenient position within the menu. For example, if you use the Excel program on a regular basis, you can place the Microsoft Excel command at the top of the Start menu. That way, when you click the Start button, you can choose the Microsoft Excel command to start Excel instantly.

To customize the Start menu, follow these steps:

1. Click the Start button and choose Settings, Taskbar. The Taskbar Properties sheet appears.

2. Click the Start Menu Programs tab, if necessary (see Figure 20.2).

3. To add an item to the Start menu, click the Add button. The Create Shortcut wizard dialog box appears. Type the path name in the Command line text box for the item you want to add. (If you don't know the path name for the item, click the Browse button to choose the path

name from the Browse dialog box.) Choose Next to
continue. Then follow the instructions in each wizard
dialog box to add an item to the Start menu.

4. To remove an item from the Start menu, click the Remove
button. Scroll through the items in the list box in the
Remove Shortcuts/Folders dialog box. To expand a folder
and view its subfolders, double-click on the folder that
contains a plus sign (+). Click the item you want to remove from the Start menu. When the item is highlighted,
that item will be removed from the Start menu. Then
click the Remove button. When you're finished removing
the items, one at a time, click the Close button to close
the Remove Shortcuts/Folders dialog box.

5. After you finish adding and removing the items, choose
OK. When you open the Start menu, you'll see the application you added at the top of the menu.

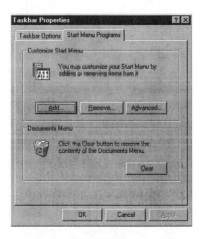

FIGURE 20.2    Customizing the Start menu in the Taskbar Properties sheet.

# CHANGING PROPERTIES

Windows 95 provides properties throughout the program that you can use to customize any object in the user interface. For example, you can rename your hard drive in the Disk Property sheet. To change the properties for a Windows object, follow these steps:

 **TIP**   **Properties**   Properties are settings for your display, files, folders, system, MS-DOS programs, and any object in Windows that you can customize to suit your needs.

1. Right-click on the object you want to change a property for. The shortcut menu appears.

2. Choose Properties and the Properties sheet appears. Figure 20.3 shows the Recycle Bin Properties sheet.

3. Make the necessary changes to the information in the Properties sheet.

4. Choose OK. The changes take effect immediately and remain until you access the property sheet and make changes again.

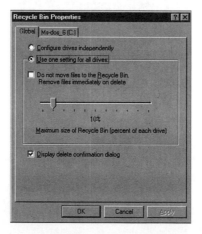

FIGURE 20.3   The Recycle Bin Properties sheet.

**Windows 95 Properties**   The properties in
Windows 95 aren't available in Windows 3.1.

In this lesson, you learned to create shortcuts, customize the Start
menu, and use properties. In the next lesson, you learn how to
run DOS applications in Windows.

# RUNNING DOS APPLICATIONS

*In this lesson, you learn to use Windows features in DOS applications, understand new DOS commands, and configure DOS applications.*

## USING THE MS-DOS PROMPT PROGRAM

The MS-DOS Prompt program icon lets you install and run DOS applications while running Windows. The MS-DOS Prompt program appears at the bottom of the Programs menu. For instructions on how to add DOS programs to the Start menu, see Lesson 20.

## USING WINDOWS FEATURES IN DOS APPLICATIONS

You can run your DOS applications under Windows 95, just as you did in Windows 3.1. There are several Windows features you can use in a DOS application, including a toolbar, a window you can size, and a Close button. These features enable you to work in a DOS application just as you would in a Windows application.

**More support for Running DOS Applications** Windows 95 provides more support for running DOS applications than Windows 3.1. Applications that wouldn't run under Windows 3.1 now run properly in Windows 95, including applications that require special hardware (such as a joystick for games). When you run a DOS application in a window under Windows 95, you can now use a toolbar and a Close button, and you can size a window.

To open a DOS program in a window, follow these steps:

1. Choose Start, Programs. The Programs menu appears.

2. Choose MS-DOS Prompt. You see the MS-DOS prompt in a window.

3. At the MS-DOS prompt, type the command that starts your MS-DOS program. The DOS program appears in a window, as shown in Figure 21.1.

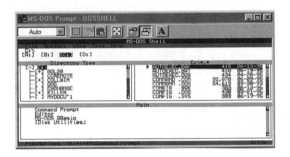

FIGURE 21.1    A DOS program in a window.

## DISPLAYING A TOOLBAR

When you run a DOS application in a window under Windows 95, a toolbar appears at the top of the window. The buttons on the toolbar provide access to the most common commands, enabling you to work with the DOS application as if it were a Windows application. You can click a button on the toolbar to quickly perform the following functions:

- Cut, copy, and paste text and graphics between DOS and Windows applications

- Switch between a window and full-screen mode

- View properties of the DOS application

- Access font options for displaying text in a DOS application window.

## SIZING A DOS WINDOW

You can change the size of a DOS application window the same way you resize a Windows 95 window—simply point to the border of the DOS application window until the mouse pointer becomes a double-headed arrow, then drag the border of the window in the direction you want to shrink or enlarge the window.

The Minimize, Maximize, and Restore buttons appear in the upper right corner of the DOS application window. These buttons are identical to the Minimize, Maximize, and Restore buttons in a Windows 95 window. Click the Minimize button in the DOS application window to change the window to a button on the taskbar. Click the Maximize button to enlarge the display to full-screen size in the window. Click the Restore button to restore the full-screen window to its previous size.

If you press **Alt+Enter**, the DOS application displays as full size without a window. When you press **Alt+Enter** again, the DOS application displays in a window again.

## USING THE CLOSE BUTTON

When you open a DOS application in a window, you'll see a Close button (the button with an X on it) in the upper-right corner of the window. This button is the same as the Close button in a Windows 95 window.

To close a DOS application, follow these steps:

1. Exit your DOS application as you normally do. You see the MS-DOS prompt.

2. Click the Close button to close the MS-DOS prompt window.

# UNDERSTANDING THE NEW DOS COMMANDS

There are new DOS commands that make it easy for you to work with DOS applications under Windows 95. For instance, the Start command enables you to access new capabilities supported by Windows 95. Also, there are commands that work with files that have long file names in Windows 95.

**New DOS Commands**   The Start command and the commands (such as Dir and Copy) that work with long file names in Windows 95 aren't available under Windows 3.1.

## THE START COMMAND

The Start command enables you to start a Windows or DOS application from the MS-DOS command prompt. To use this command, follow these steps:

1. Choose Start, Programs. Then choose the MS-DOS Prompt program. The MS-DOS window appears.

2. At the MS-DOS prompt, type **start**, press the **spacebar**, then type the application name. For example, type **start excel**. If you want to start an application and open a document, type the document name and file type. For example, type **start budget.xls**.

**It Won't Start**   If the program doesn't start, type it in again including the path. For example, to start the Norton Utilities, type Start C:\NU\Norton. You can also edit the path in the AUTOEXEC.BAT file.

## Long File Names

You can now use long file names in Windows 95 and in DOS applications that run under Windows 95. There are several commands in DOS that work with files that have long file names. For example, the DIR command shows long file names as well as the corresponding 8.3 file name (a file name with a maximum of 8 characters and a 3 character extension indicating file type). You can also display additional file details with the DIR command. To do so, type **dir/v**. (The v stands for verbose mode.) The additional file details include the file name, file type, file size, allocated space, last modified date and time, last accessed date, and attributes such as D for directory and A for archived.

The COPY command also supports long file names. You can copy to or from short or long file names. You must precede the long file name with a double quote ("). For example, type **copy budget.xls "annual budget**. This example creates a new file with a long file name.

# Configuring DOS Applications

DOS applications have properties just like Windows applications do. You can configure DOS applications by changing the information in a DOS application property sheet. There are several tabs in the Property sheet that allow you to change options related to the following elements: Program, Font, Memory, Screen, and Misc. To view properties for a DOS application, follow these steps:

**MS-DOS Properties**   MS-DOS properties contain settings that control the objects for your DOS application in a window. You can change these settings at any time by right-clicking on the object you want to change and choosing Properties. You can change the program, font, memory, screen, and miscellaneous properties for a DOS application in a window.

1. Click the Properties button on the MS-DOS Prompt toolbar at the top of the MS-DOS prompt window. The Properties sheet appears.

2. Click the appropriate tab to see the options you want to change. For example, click the Screen tab to change the screen settings for the MS-DOS prompt window.

3. Make the necessary changes to the properties information. For example, by default, the MS-DOS Prompt toolbar displays at the top of the MS-DOS prompt window. Choose the Display Toolbar option to remove the toolbar from the window. Then click OK.

In this lesson, you learned to run DOS programs under Windows. In the next lesson, you learn how to create a document in WordPad.

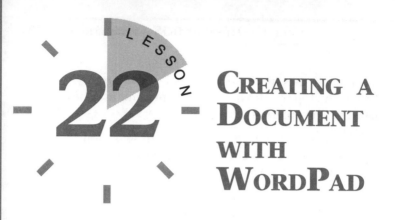

# CREATING A DOCUMENT WITH WORDPAD

*In this lesson, you learn to create, edit, save, preview, and print a document in WordPad.*

## CREATING A DOCUMENT

You can use Windows 95's WordPad program to create any document. For example, you can create letters, memos, reports, lists, newsletters, and so on. To create a document, follow these steps:

1. Choose Start, Programs, Accessories, then select WordPad. WordPad displays a blank document on-screen (see Figure 22.1).

2. Start typing your text.

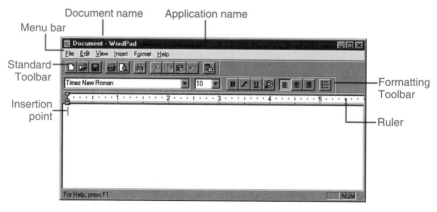

**FIGURE 22.1** The Windows 95 WordPad window.

When entering text in a WordPad document, don't press Enter at the end of each line. WordPad automatically begins a new line when you fill up the previous one. Press **Enter** only to mark the end of a paragraph.

The WordPad screen contains the following elements:

- Application name (**WordPad**)

- Document name (**Document** for now; you assign a name when you save the document)

- The menu bar containing the WordPad menus

- The text insertion point, which marks the location that the text you enter is placed

- Standard Toolbar for quick selection of WordPad commands

- Formatting Toolbar for quick selection of formatting commands

- A ruler to change tabs and margins

 **Word Processor**   The WordPad program in Windows 95 replaces the Write program in Windows 3.1.

# EDITING YOUR DOCUMENT

Everyone makes mistakes. When you do, you can easily edit your document. The following sections show you how. For information on selecting text or copying and moving text, refer to Lesson 9.

## MOVING THE TEXT INSERTION POINT

To move the insertion point with the mouse, just click the place you want to move it to. To move the insertion point using the keyboard, see the options in Table 22.1. You can use these keys without disturbing existing text.

**TABLE 22.1    MOVING THE INSERTION POINT WITH THE KEYBOARD**

| PRESS | TO MOVE |
|---|---|
| ⬇ | Down one line |
| ⬆ | Up one line |
| ➡ | Right one character |
| ⬅ | Left one character |
| PageUp | Previous screen |
| PageDown | Next screen |
| Ctrl+➡ | Next word |
| Ctrl+⬅ | Previous word |
| Ctrl+PageUp | Top of screen |
| Ctrl+PageDown | Bottom of screen |
| Home | Beginning of line |
| End | End of line |
| Ctrl+Home | Beginning of document |
| Ctrl+End | End of document |

## INSERTING TEXT

To insert text within existing characters, simply place the insertion point in the appropriate location (using the mouse or the keyboard) and begin typing. The characters move to the right as you type.

## DELETING TEXT

To delete a single character, press the **Backspace** key to delete the character to the left. Press the **Delete** key to delete the character to the right. To delete larger amounts of text, select the text and press the **Delete** key.

# FORMATTING YOUR DOCUMENT

You can affect the appearance of your document on-screen and when printed by changing the formatting. Formatting refers to the appearance of a document, including font, font style, and font size, as well as text alignment.

## FONT, FONT STYLE, AND FONT SIZE

You can change the following text attributes to improve the appearance of your text or set it apart from other text:

- **Font**   Aria, Times New Roman, MS Sans Serif, and so on

- **Font Style**   Bold, Italic, and Underline

- **Font Size**   10-point, 12-point, and 20-point. (There are approximately 72 points in an inch.)

**What's a Font?**   In WordPad, a font is a set of characters that have the same typeface, for example, Helvetica. When you select a font, WordPad allows you to change the font's size, add an optional attribute to the font, such as bold or italic; and underline the text.

To change the font, font style, and font size:

1. Choose Format, Font in the WordPad menu bar. The Font dialog box appears (see Figure 22.2).

2. Select the font, font style, and font size options you want. To underline text, select the Underline option. The Sample area shows sample text with the options you selected.

3. Choose OK to apply the font changes.

Font Style

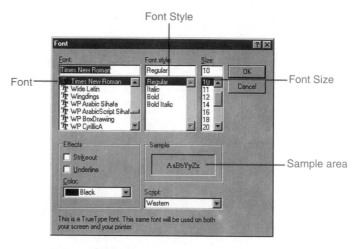

Font

Font Size

Sample area

FIGURE 22.2    The font options in the Font dialog box.

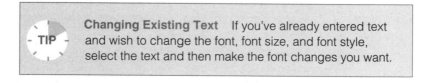

**Changing Existing Text**  If you've already entered text and wish to change the font, font size, and font style, select the text and then make the font changes you want.

Figure 22.3 shows a document after different attributes have been changed for selected text.

Boldface
16-point
Times New Roman

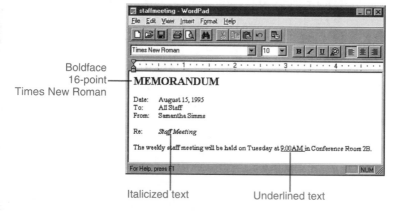

Italicized text            Underlined text

FIGURE 22.3    Sample text attributes.

## TEXT ALIGNMENT

Normally, text is aligned with the left margin. However, you can right-align text or center the text between the margins.

To align text:

1. Choose Format, Paragraph in the WordPad menu bar. The Paragraph dialog box appears.

2. Click the drop-down arrow next to the Alignment option. Select the alignment option you want.

3. Choose OK to apply the alignment change.

You also can use the Formatting toolbar in the WordPad window to change the text attributes and align text. To apply text attributes and align text using the Formatting toolbar, see the options in Table 22.2.

**TABLE 22.2   TEXT ATTRIBUTE AND ALIGNMENT BUTTONS ON THE FORMATTING TOOLBAR**

| CLICK | TO APPLY |
|-------|----------|
| **B** | Bold |
| *I* | Italic |
| U | Underline |
| ≣ | Left alignment |
| ≣ | Center alignment |
| ≣ | Right alignment |

# Saving the WordPad Document

Whether you're creating a WordPad document or another type of document file, save your work often. To save a WordPad document, follow these steps:

1. Choose File, Save.

2. If the document hasn't been saved before, the Save As dialog box (shown in Figure 22.4) appears. From the Save In box, select the folder in which you want to save the document. Then, in the File Name text box, enter the name you want to assign to the document. WordPad automatically assigns the .DOC extension to files created in WordPad. WordPad documents are automatically saved in Word for Windows 6.0 format. Click Save.

If the document has been saved before, WordPad simply saves the changes you made.

3. Once the document is saved, you're returned to the document window to either continue working or to exit. Notice the file name appears in the title bar.

**TIP**

**Saving a Document Under a New Name**   Use the File, Save As command to save a copy of the document under a different name or as a different file type.

**Figure 22.4**   The dialog box for saving a new document.

Notice in Figure 22.4, the Windows folder is selected (the file folder symbol appears to be open and the files in the folder appear in the list). When you select Save, the file **SWIMMEMO** is saved to the Windows folder.

**Better Saved Than Sorry**   When in doubt, save your document. It's better to save often than to risk losing hours of effort.

# PRINTING THE WORDPAD DOCUMENT

Once your document is complete, you can print it. You can preview the document before printing it. Simply follow these steps:

 1. Click the Print Preview button on the WordPad toolbar. The Print Preview window appears (see Figure 22.5).

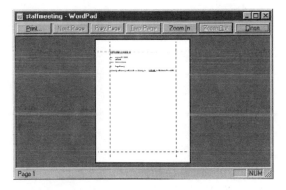

**FIGURE 22.5**   The Print Preview window.

2. Click the Zoom In button on the Print Preview toolbar to magnify your document. When you're finished viewing the document, click the Close button on the Print Preview toolbar. You are returned to the document.

3. Choose File, Print. The Print dialog box appears.

4. Identify the number of copies you want (if it's more than one) and the pages to print (if applicable), then click OK.

5. A dialog box appears to let you know the document is printing. To cancel the print job, click Cancel.

In this lesson, you learned the basics of using WordPad, the word-processing program included with Windows. The next lesson shows you the basics of using Paint, the graphics program included with Windows.

# ADDING GRAPHICS WITH PAINT

*In this lesson, you learn to open and draw with Paint, add text to your drawing, and save and print your drawing.*

## OPENING PAINT

Paint allows you to give your documents an artistic touch. You can create everything from free-flowing drawings to precise mathematical charts. For example, you can illustrate a story, emphasize an important point in a report, or clarify instructions. Your creations can be used in other Windows applications such as Windows WordPad or Word for Windows.

To open a Paint document, follow these steps:

1. Choose Start, Programs, Accessories.

2. Select the Paint program. The Paint window shown in Figure 23.1 appears.

In addition to the standard application window parts, the Paint window shown in Figure 23.1 also has a set of drawing tools (called the *toolbox*) on the left and a *color palette* at the bottom of the window.

**Background and Foreground Colors**   The box within a box to the left of the color palette shows the currently selected foreground and background colors. The foreground color is the color you'll use when you draw, and the background color is the color of the backdrop.

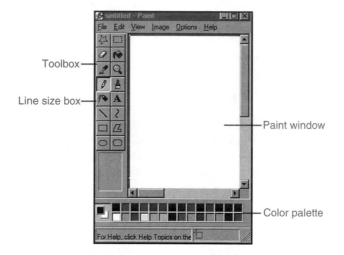

Toolbox

Line size box

Paint window

Color palette

**FIGURE 23.1**   The Windows 95 Paint window.

The line size box on the lower left of the window identifies the width of a line and the options for the currently selected tool in the toolbox. Figure 23.2 shows each of the tools in the toolbox.

 **Paint**   The Paint program in Windows 95 replaces the Paintbrush program in Windows 3.1.

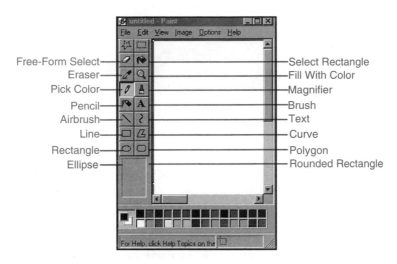

FIGURE 23.2    The tools in the toolbox.

# DRAWING IN PAINT

Although it's possible to use the keyboard to draw objects, it's much easier to use the mouse. Follow these steps to draw:

1. To select the background color, point at a color in the color palette and click the right mouse button.

2. To select the foreground color, point at the color in the color palette and click the left mouse button.

3. To select the size of the drawing, choose Image, Attributes, and enter the Width and Height in the Attributes dialog box (see Figure 23.3). Click OK.

FIGURE 23.3    The Attributes dialog box.

4. Choose File, New to open a new document with the settings you entered in steps 1-3.

5. Select a drawing tool from the toolbox at the left of the screen.

6. To select a line width, click the line size you want in the Line Style box in the lower left of the screen.

7. To draw an object, point at the area where you want the object to appear, press and hold the left mouse button, and drag the mouse pointer until the object is the size you desire.

**Oops!**    If you add to your graphic and decide you don't like the addition, choose Edit, Undo (or press **Ctrl+Z**) to undo the change you made. Use this option carefully, however, because all changes you've made since you last changed tools will be undone.

**A Perfect Circle Every Time**    To draw a perfect circle, select the Ellipse tool, hold down the **Shift** key, and click and drag the mouse pointer. You can also use this technique to draw a perfect square with the Rectangle tool and a perfectly straight line with the Line tool.

# ADDING TEXT TO A GRAPHIC

To add text to a graphic, follow these steps:

1. Select the Text tool.

2. Click in the drawing where you want the text to go and drag the mouse pointer diagonally to draw a text frame. The Text toolbar appears when you release the mouse button.

3. On the Text toolbar, select the Font, Size, and Style you want for the text. If desired, click the Close button on the Text toolbar to close the toolbar.

4. Click inside the text frame where you want to begin entering text.

5. Type the text, then click outside the text frame to insert the text.

> **Once You Leave, You Can Never Get Back**  You can't edit text once you've accepted it; you can only erase it. To erase the text, select the text frame and press **Delete**. Because of this, be sure what you've typed is correct before you move on.

# SAVING THE DRAWING

To save the drawing, follow these steps:

1. Choose File, Save. The Save As dialog box appears.

2. If you want to change the file type, choose a file type from the Save as Type drop-down list box in the Save As dialog box.

3. Choose a folder from the Folder list to save the drawing in, type the name of the drawing in the File Name text box, and select Save. When you save this drawing in the future, the Save As dialog box won't appear. If you need to access this dialog box again, choose File, Save As.

# PRINTING THE DRAWING

To print the drawing:

1. Choose File, Print. The Print dialog box appears.

2. Complete the Print dialog box.

3. Click OK.

In this lesson, you learned to use Windows' Paint accessory. In the next lesson, you learn to use two more accessories, HyperTerminal and Phone Dialer.

# USING THE OTHER ACCESSORIES

*In this lesson, you learn to use HyperTerminal Connections and Phone Dialer.*

## USING HYPERTERMINAL CONNECTIONS

The HyperTerminal Connections program lets you connect to a remote computer that isn't running under Windows. You can use HyperTerminal and your modem to send and receive files or connect to a mainframe, a computer bulletin board, or another PC. To use HyperTerminal, follow these steps:

1. Choose Start, Programs, Accessories.

2. Click on HyperTerminal. The HyperTerminal window appears.

FIGURE 24.1   The Windows 95 HyperTerminal window.

3. Double-click on Hypertrm. The Connection Description dialog box appears. If you already set up a connection, click Cancel in the Connection Description dialog box.

4. If you haven't set up a connection, in the Connection Description dialog box, enter a name for the connection in the Name text box. Then choose an icon for the connection in the Icon list box. Click OK.

5. In the Phone Number dialog box, enter the phone number and other calling information. Click OK.

6. Choose File, Open from the HyperTerminal menu bar. The Open dialog box appears.

7. Double-click on the connection in the list box that you want to use.

8. Choose Call, Connect from the HyperTerminal menu bar. Then click the Dial button to call the remote computer.

9. After the connection is made and when you're finished using HyperTerminal, Windows prompts you to save the session.

 **HyperTerminal**   The HyperTerminal program in Windows 95 replaces the Terminal program in Windows 3.1.

## USING THE PHONE DIALER

The Phone Dialer program enables you to place phone calls from your computer by using your modem or another Windows telephone device. You can dial another computer modem's phone number and make a connection. To use Phone Dialer, follow these steps:

1. Choose Start, Programs, Accessories.

2. Click Phone Dialer. The Phone Dialer appears (see Figure 24.2).

FIGURE 24.2    The Windows 95 Phone Dialer.

3. Type a phone number in the Number to Dial text box or click a phone number in the Number to Dial list box you already dialed. Then click Dial. You can also click on a Speed Dial button to dial the phone number.

To store a frequently used phone number, click an empty Speed Dial button and the Program Speed Dial dialog box appears. Enter the information requested, and click Save or Save And Dial.

 **Phone Dialer**   The Phone Dialer program in Windows 95 replaces the Phone Dial command in the Terminal program in Windows 3.1.

In this lesson, you learned how to use HyperTerminal Connections and Phone Dialer. In the next lesson, you learn how to control multimedia with Windows.

# WORKING WITH MULTIMEDIA

*In this les-                    son, you learn to use CD Player, Media Player, Sound Recorder, and Volume Control to work with multimedia.*

## USING THE CD PLAYER

Windows 95 provides a built-in CD Player so you can play audio CDs while you're working. This CD Player contains features just like a regular advanced CD player, such as random play, programmable playback order, and the capability to save programs. If you save a program, you don't have to recreate the play list each time you insert a CD. That way, you can skip over songs you don't want to play. To use the CD Player, follow these steps:

1. Choose Start, Programs, Accessories.

2. Choose Multimedia, CD Player. The CD Player window appears (see Figure 25.1). When you insert a compact disc, the CD Player launches and begins playback automatically.

3. Insert a CD in your CD-ROM drive. The CD's artist, title, and track appear in the CD Player window if you've entered this information before.

4. To set up a play list, choose File, Edit Play List on the CD Player menu bar. The Edit Play List dialog box appears. Specify which tracks you want to play and in which order. Click Add to add each track to the play list. Click Set Name to save a program.

5. Click the Play button in the CD Player window to play
the CD. To pause the CD, click the Pause button. To resume playing the CD, click the Play button. To play the
CD in random order, choose Options, Random Order on
the CD Player menu bar.

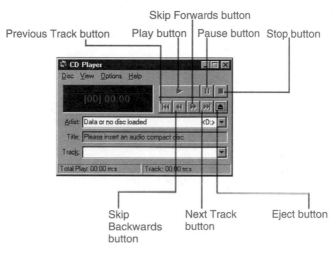

FIGURE 25.1   The Windows 95 CD Player window.

**Change Tracks**   Click the Previous Track button to play
the previous track. Click the Next Track button to play the
next track.

**Skip Around**   Click the Skip Backwards button to move
backward within a track. Click the Skip Forwards button to
move forward within a track.

6. Click the Stop button to stop playing your CD.

7. Click the Eject button to eject your CD.

**CD Player**   The CD Player program in Windows 95 isn't
available in Windows 3.1.

# USING THE MEDIA PLAYER

The Media Player program enables you to play multimedia files
such as Windows-compatible multimedia voice, animated video
files, and MIDI-based music files. Windows supports the following
digital video file formats: .AVI, .BMP, .PCX, .TXT, .WAV, and
.WRI. If you don't have a CD-ROM drive, you can use the Media
Player to play your CDs.

**MIDI file**   A MIDI file contains electronic instructions for
playing a song and can be compared to sheet music. A
device such as a sound card can play the song contained in a MIDI file. Musicians can use MIDI as a development tool to control music equipment and add music to
titles and games. Windows 95 supports MIDI and wave-
form audio .WAV files.

To use the Media Player, follow these steps:

1. Choose Start, Programs, Accessories.

2. Choose Multimedia, Media Player. The Media Player window appears (see Figure 25.2).

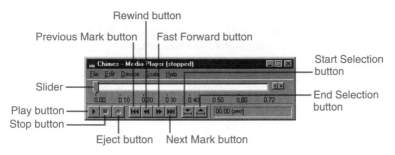

**FIGURE 25.2**    The Windows 95 Media Player window.

3. Choose Device from the Media Player menu bar and select the device you want to play. The Open dialog box
   appears.

4. Double-click the file you want to play.

5. Click the Play button in the Media Player window to play
   the file.

**Rewind and Fast Forward**    Drag the slider to the left to
rewind to the previous selection mark or to the beginning
of the file. Drag the slider to the right to fast forward to the
next selection mark or to the end of the file.

6. Click the Stop button to stop playing your file.

7. Click the Eject button to eject your file.

To play a specific selection, move the slider to the location where
you want to start playing the selection. Click the Start Selection
button to mark the beginning of the selection. Move the slider to
the location where you want to stop playing the selection. Click
the End Selection button to mark the end of the selection. Press
**Alt+P** and then click the Play button to perform the selection
you specified.

**Media Player**   The Media Player program in Windows 95 is similar to the Media Player program in Windows 3.1. Windows 95's AutoPlay feature makes it easier for you to install and run audio CD-ROMs. When you put a Windows 95 audio CD disk into a CD-ROM drive, Windows automatically spins the disk, opens it, and follows the setup instructions.

# USING THE SOUND RECORDER

The Sound Recorder program lets you record, modify, and mix sounds. To play a sound using the Sound Recorder, follow these steps:

1. Choose Start, Programs, Accessories.

2. Choose Multimedia, Sound Recorder. The Sound Recorder window appears (see Figure 25.3).

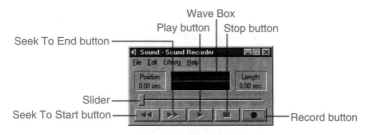

**FIGURE 25.3**   The Windows 95 Sound Recorder window.

3. Choose File, Open from the Sound Recorder menu bar. The Open dialog box appears.

4. Double-click the sound file you want to play.

5. Click the Play button in the Sound Recorder window to play the sound. As the sound plays, you see a visual representation of the sound waves in the Wave box.

To be able to record sounds you must have some type of input device such as a microphone or a MIDI instrument. You must also have a sound card, even if you're just recording a CD to a file.

To record a sound, follow these steps:

1. Choose File, New from the Sound Recorder menu bar. The New Sound dialog box appears.

2. Enter a name for the sound file and specify the file format and attributes. Choose OK.

3. Click the Record button to begin recording.

4. Speak into the microphone to record the message.

5. When you're finished recording, click the Stop button to stop recording.

6. Choose File, Save As from the Sound Recorder menu bar to save the sound file.

You can edit sounds by adding effects and mixing sounds together. Choose the Options menu on the Sound Recorder menu bar to add affects. Choose Edit, Mix File to mix sounds. The following effects are available:

- Increase volume by 25%

- Decrease volume

- Increase speed by 100%

- Decrease speed

- Add echo

- Reverse

 **Sound Recorder**    The Sound Recorder program in Windows 95 and Windows 3.1 work the same way.

# USING VOLUME CONTROL

The Volume Control program enables you to control the balance between the left and right speakers, adjust the volume, and turn the sound off for all multimedia devices. To use Volume Control, follow these steps:

1. Choose Start, Programs, Accessories.

2. Choose Multimedia, Volume Control. The Volume Control window appears (see Figure 25.4).

Balance

Volume

Mute

**FIGURE 25.4**   The Windows 95 Volume Control window.

3. For Volume Control, Wave, MIDI, CD, or Line-in, drag the Balance slider bar left and right to balance the sound between the left and right speakers.

4. For Volume Control, Wave, MIDI, CD, or Line-in, drag the Volume slider bar up or down to increase or decrease the volume.

5. For Volume Control, Wave, MIDI, CD, or Line-in, click the Mute check box to turn the sound off. An X appears in the Mute check box, indicating that the sound is turned off. To turn the sound on, click the Mute check box to remove the X in the check box.

**TIP**

**Adjusting Volume**   The Volume Control button appears on the taskbar. If you click on the taskbar's Volume Control, you can turn the sound up or down easily. If you double-click on the taskbar's Volume Control, you see the Volume Control dialog box.

**Volume Control**    The Volume Control program in Windows 95 isn't available in Windows 3.1.

In this lesson, you learned to use CD Player, Media Player, Sound Recorder, and Volume Control. In the next lesson, you learn to use Disk Defragmenter, ScanDisk, and DriveSpace.

# 26 LESSON
## Maintaining Windows 95 with the Tools Programs

*In this lesson, you learn to use Disk Defragmenter, DriveSpace, and ScanDisk.*

## Using Disk Defragmenter

The Disk Defragmenter program lets you free up space on your hard disk by rearranging files and unused space on the disk to make your programs run faster. To use the Disk Defragmenter, follow these steps:

1. Choose Start, Programs, Accessories.

2. Choose System Tools, Disk Defragmenter. The Select Drive window appears (see Figure 26.1).

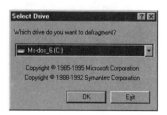

**Figure 26.1** The Select Drive window.

3. Choose the drive you want to defragment. For example, choose Drive C. You can't defragment a CD-ROM, network drive, or compressed drive that wasn't compressed with a Windows compression program.

**4.** Choose OK to begin defragmenting your disk.

 **Disk Defragmenter** The Disk Defragmenter program in Windows 95 isn't available in Windows 3.1.

# USING DRIVESPACE

After you use Disk Defragmenter to free up disk space, use DriveSpace to increase your disk space. DriveSpace enables you to compress hard and floppy disks to make more free space for your files. To use DriveSpace, follow these steps:

**1.** Choose Start, Programs, Accessories.

**2.** Choose System Tools, DriveSpace. The DriveSpace window appears (see Figure 26.2).

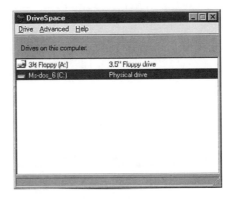

**FIGURE 26.2**    The DriveSpace window.

**3.** Choose the disk you want to compress.

**4.** Choose Drive, Compress. The Compress a Drive dialog box appears. Windows displays the amount of free and used space, and the drive's capacity before and after compression.

**5.** Click the Start button to begin compressing the drive.

6. If you have not backed up your drive, click Back Up Files and follow the instructions to back up your files.

7. Click Compress Now to compress the drive. If Windows asks you to restart the computer, click Yes.

 **DriveSpace** The DriveSpace program in Windows 95 replaces the DoubleSpace program in MS-DOS 6.0 and 6.2 and the DriveSpace program in MS-DOS 6.22. If you already used DoubleSpace or DriveSpace to compress your disks, you can still use Windows 95's DriveSpace to compress your disks.

# Using ScanDisk

The ScanDisk program lets you check your hard disk for disk errors and then repair the damage to the disk. To use ScanDisk, follow these steps:

1. Choose Start, Programs, Accessories.

2. Choose System Tools, ScanDisk. The ScanDisk window appears (see Figure 26.3).

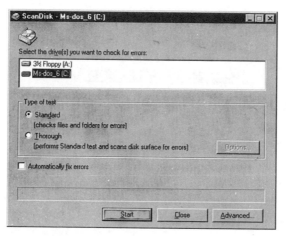

**Figure 26.3** The ScanDisk window.

3. Select the drive you want to check for errors.

4. Choose the type of test you want to run. Choose the Standard option if you want to check your files and folders for errors. Choose the Thorough option to perform the Standard test and scan the disk surface for errors.

5. If you want Windows 95 to automatically repair the damage after finding the errors, click the Automatically Fix Errors check box.

6. Click the Start button to begin checking the disk for errors. If you didn't choose the Automatically Fix Errors option, you will be prompted to specify how you want an error fixed when ScanDisk finds an error.

 **ScanDisk** The ScanDisk program in Windows 95 isn't available in Windows 3.1.

In this lesson, you learned how to use Disk Defragmenter, DriveSpace, and ScanDisk. The following appendixes provide information for people who are upgrading from Windows 3.1 and people who are using Windows 95 on a network.

# UPGRADER'S HELP

| WINDOWS 3.1<br>FEATURE OR TASK | WINDOWS 95<br>FEATURE OR TASK |
|---|---|
| Adding a printer | Add a printer with the Add Printer Wizard by choosing the Add icon in the Printers folder. |
| Arranging icons | The Auto Arrange command works the same way. Also, you can use the Arrange Icons command to sort the items in the window by Name and Description. |
| Browsing | Browsing through folders and windows in Windows 95 is a new feature. |
| Clock | Works the same way. |
| Closing a window | Instead of double-clicking the Control menu, you click the Close button. |
| Control menu | Now an application icon instead of a file drawer icon. |
| Control Panel | The Mouse, Keyboard, and Date/Time icons in the Control Panel are the same. Add New Hardware, Add/Remove |

| WINDOWS 3.1 FEATURE OR TASK | WINDOWS 95 FEATURE OR TASK |
|---|---|
| | Programs, Joystick, Multimedia, Passwords, Regional Settings, and System are new. |
| Control Panel, Color | The Display icon in the Control Panel replaces the Color icon in the Control Panel. |
| Control Panel, Desktop | The Display icon in the Control Panel replaces the Color and Desktop icons in the Control Panel. |
| Control Panel, Drivers | The Add New Hardware icon replaces the Drivers icon in the Control Panel. |
| Control Panel, International Settings | The Regional Settings icon replaces the International Settings icon in the Control Panel. |
| Control Panel, Printers | The Printers Folder replaces the Printers icon in the Control Panel. |
| Control Panel, Sound | The Multimedia and Sounds icons replace the Sound icon in the Control Panel. |
| Copy command | Works the same way. |
| Creating new file icons | In Windows 95, Windows creates file icons for programs automatically, whereas in Windows 3.1, you create your own file icons for programs. |

*continues*

*continued*

| WINDOWS 3.1 FEATURE OR TASK | WINDOWS 95 FEATURE OR TASK |
| --- | --- |
| Cut command | Works the same way. |
| Deleting a file or directory | You see only the Confirm Delete dialog box instead of seeing both the Delete dialog box and the Confirm Delete dialog box. |
| Deleting directories | You now delete folders, but it works the same way. |
| Desktop | My Computer icon, Recycle Bin icon, Start button, taskbar. |
| Dialog boxes | Work the same way. |
| Directories | Folders replace directories. |
| DOS System Tools | The DriveSpace program replaces the DoubleSpace program in MS-DOS 6.0 and 6.2 and the DriveSpace program in MS-DOS 6.22. The Disk DeFragmenter and ScanDisk programs are new. |
| Exiting Windows applications | Handled the same way except there's a Close button in Windows 95 application windows. |
| File Manager | Windows Explorer replaces File Manager. |
| File, Copy command | Edit, Copy command. Also, the Copy and confirmation dialog boxes no longer appear when you copy files and folders. |

| WINDOWS 3.1 FEATURE OR TASK | WINDOWS 95 FEATURE OR TASK |
| --- | --- |
| File, Create Directory command | File, New Folder command. |
| File, Move command | Edit, Cut command. Also, the Move confirmation dialog box no longer appears when you move files and folders. |
| File names | File names can have up to 255 characters (including spaces) and don't require a file extension. |
| Help | Help is organized differently. Windows 95 has three main functions: Contents, Index, and Find. You no longer have to scroll the Help window because the Help topics are short and they fit in one small screen. |
| Installing and removing fonts | Install and remove fonts with the Fonts folder in the Control Panel. |
| Maximize button/command | The Maximize command works the same way, but has a new look. |
| Menus | Menus cascade automatically as the mouse pointer passes over them. |
| Minimize button/command | The Minimize command in Windows 95 decreases the window to a button on the taskbar. The Minimize button has a new look. |

*continues*

*continued*

| WINDOWS 3.1 FEATURE OR TASK | WINDOWS 95 FEATURE OR TASK |
| --- | --- |
| Mouse basics | Mouse actions are the same in Windows 95 except you can click the right mouse button as a shortcut for the most common tasks you perform in Windows 95. |
| Moving a window | Works the same way. |
| Multimedia | The Media Player and Sound Recorder accessories work the same way. The CD Player and Volume Control accessories are new. |
| Notepad | Works the same. |
| Opening a window | Works the same. |
| Paintbrush | The Paint program replaces the Paintbrush program. |
| Paste | Works the same way. |
| Print Manager | Printers Folder. Each individual printer in the Printers Folder handles its own print jobs. |
| Program Manager | Start menu. |
| Renaming files or directories | You type the new name next to the icon instead of typing the new name into the Rename dialog box. |
| Restarting the computer | Use the Restart the computer option in the Shutdown Windows dialog box in Windows 95 to restart the |

| WINDOWS 3.1 FEATURE OR TASK | WINDOWS 95 FEATURE OR TASK |
| --- | --- |
| | computer. You can also press Ctrl+Alt+Del to restart Windows 95 and then choose Shut Down from the Close Program dialog box. |
| Restore button/command | Has a new look; works the same way. |
| Run command | Works the same way. |
| Scroll bars | The scroll bars appear sculpted in Windows 95. The size of the scroll box within the scroll bar depicts how much of a window is not visible. |
| Search command | The Find command. |
| Selecting files or directories | Works the same way. |
| Sizing borders | Works the same way. |
| Starting Windows | Windows 95 starts automatically when you turn on your computer. (You no longer have to type WIN and press Enter.) |
| Starting Windows applications | Single-click icons in Windows 95 to start a program using Start, Programs. Double-click icons in Windows 95 to start a program from My Computer, Control Panel, or Windows Explorer. |

*continues*

*continued*

| Windows 3.1<br>Feature or Task | Windows 95<br>Feature or Task |
| --- | --- |
| Switching between applications | The taskbar replaces the Window menu command. When you press Alt+Tab to switch to an application, you see icons and application names in the dialog box. |
| Task List | Taskbar. |
| Terminal | The HyperTerminal and Phone Dialer programs replace the Terminal program and Phone Dial command in the Terminal program. |
| Title bar | Looks different. The title appears on the left side of the title bar. |
| View All Files command | View Details command. |
| View Partial Details command | View List command. |
| View Sort command | View Arrange Icons command. |
| Window Refresh command | View, Refresh command. |
| Write | The WordPad program replaces the Write program. |

# NETWORKING

*Windows 95 makes many advance-
ments in the area of networking. This
appendix highlights some of the most
important changes.*

## MULTIPLE NETWORK SUPPORT

Windows 95 provides support for Novell NetWare and continued built-in support for the Microsoft network. You can
install one or both networks by double-clicking the
Windows 95 Setup program or the Network icon in the Control
Panel.

## MICROSOFT CLIENT FOR NETWARE

Windows 95's Microsoft Client for NetWare enables you to operate under NetWare 3.x and 4.x servers. You can use all NetWare
server services, browse NetWare servers, and connect to servers.
You can also queue print jobs using the Windows 95 network user
interface or Novell's NetWare command line utilities. In addition,
you can run "TSR clean" NetWare login scripts to determine what
name you used to log in. Windows 95 also provides continued
support for Novell NetWare real-mode components, including the
NetWare 3.x NetX shell and 4.x VLM shell. There is also RIPL
support for tools used for setting up and booting diskless worksta-
tions from servers running NetWare services.

## MICROSOFT FILE AND PRINT SHARING
## FOR NETWARE

Windows 95 provides NetWare-compatible peer services for file
and print sharing by using the existing user-level security built
into NetWare. The Microsoft Network allows you to operate with

other Windows 95 PCs, as well as PCs running Windows for
Workgroups, Windows NT, Windows NT Advanced Server, LAN
Manager, and any other Microsoft-compatible servers. Windows
95 also provides support for client access and peer services capabilities on a Microsoft Network. Other third-party network servers
and services such as ArtiSoft, Banyan, DEC, and SunSelect will
also work under Windows 95.

# NETWORK NEIGHBORHOOD

Windows 95's Network Neighborhood is a new user interface that
makes it easier to perform common network operations on several
different servers from Windows 95. The network manager estab-
lishes one password to log the user into the Windows 95 PC and
any network resources or services to which they are entitled access
(such as e-mail, group scheduling applications, dial-in support,
and database access).

No matter what type of server Windows 95 is connected to,
common network actions such as browsing servers, managing connections, and printing are all done identically through
Windows 95. You don't have to memorize any new network commands; just use the mouse to double-click the Network Neighborhood icon on the Windows 95 desktop and perform any of the
common network actions. For example, you can locate, connect,
and start a print job on a NetWare print server just as easily as
you can for a printer attached to a Windows NT Advanced Server.

When opening the Network Neighborhood window, you see
only the servers you have logged into or the servers to which you
most frequently connect. The files and documents residing on
other PCs on the network appear in the Network Neighborhood
window.

The custom Network Neighborhood enables you to allow
shortcuts or links in the Network Neighborhood. You have
control over what does and doesn't display in the Network
Neighborhood.

# MOBILE NETWORK SUPPORT

Windows 95 makes it easier for mobile PC users with computers equipped with a PnP BIOS to connect to a network. Plug and Play and Remote Access are technologies built in to your computer's BIOS that allow Windows to detect the network configurations on your computer.

With Plug and Play, you no longer have to maintain multiple configurations, such as desktop and portable configuration, because Windows 95 recognizes when peripherals are added or removed from the network. For example, Windows 95 detects when you remove a network card and add a modem for dial-in network access.

You no longer have to reboot your system each time you make a change to the configuration. Windows 95 also supports built-in Card and Socket Services, which let you remove and insert PCMCIA cards (including network cards) while the network is running.

Plug and Play supports applications that are network-aware and understands when the network is available. If you remove the network adapter, the application automatically puts itself into "offline" mode and allows you to continue to work, or the application closes without damaging your work.

Remote Access provides modular support for multiple dial-in providers, which include Windows NT RAS servers and NetWare. Remote Access also supports the NetBEUI, IPX/SPX, and TCP/IP via PPP protocols. Third-party support for dial-in is offered for Windows 95's Remote Access, including Shiva.

PPP Stack now works better with Windows NT and Internet servers. For example, compression and encryption over PPP have been improved. The user interface (UI) has been greatly improved. For instance, a new dialer application from the TAPI group makes it easier to install a modem and dial from applications. The shell is also slow-link aware. You will also see modem lights blinking on the taskbar.

# THE MICROSOFT EXCHANGE

 The Microsoft Exchange lets you access, exchange, and organize information in a single location. When you click the Inbox icon on the Windows 95 desktop, you see the Inbox Microsoft Exchange window (see Figure B.1). This window can contain e-mail messages, forms, documents, and folders that have been stored by some information service (such as an e-mail system, workgroup application, or commercial online service).

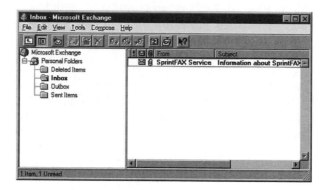

**FIGURE B.1**   The Inbox Microsoft Exchange window.

The Microsoft Exchange enables you to send and receive e-mail messages and faxes, move messages and documents between folders, and organize various types of information.

To send a fax with Microsoft Fax:

 1. Double-click the Inbox icon on the desktop. The Inbox Microsoft Exchange window appears.

2. Choose Compose, New Fax on the Microsoft Exchange menu bar. The Compose New Fax wizard dialog box appears (see Figure B.2).

3. Verify that the location that appears in the I'm Dialing From text box is correct. Then click the Next button to continue.

4. Follow the instructions in the rest of the Compose New Fax dialog boxes to send your fax.

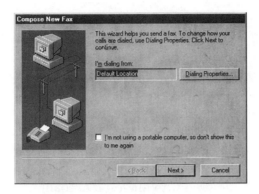

FIGURE B.2    The Compose New Fax dialog box.

To receive a fax with Microsoft Fax:

 1. Double-click the Inbox icon on the desktop. The Inbox
Microsoft Exchange window appears.

 2. Click the Fax Machine icon that appears between the
Volume Control icon and the time on the taskbar. The
Microsoft Fax Status dialog box appears (see Figure B.3).

FIGURE B.3    The Microsoft Fax Status dialog box.

3. Click the Answer Now button to receive the fax.

To read e-Mail with Microsoft Exchange:

 1. Double-click the Inbox icon on the desktop. The Inbox
Microsoft Exchange window appears.

2. Click the Inbox button on the Microsoft Exchange
toolbar. Your new mail appears in a list in the window.

3. Double-click on the message you want to read. The message displays in the window.

4. If you want to reply to the sender of the message, click the Reply to Sender button on the Microsoft Exchange toolbar.

5. Type your message in the Reply to Sender dialog box. Then click the Send button on the Reply to Sender toolbar to send the message.

6. If you want to delete a message, select the message and then click the Delete button on the Microsoft Exchange toolbar.

To send e-mail messages with Microsoft Exchange:

1. Double-click the Inbox icon on the desktop. The Inbox Microsoft Exchange window appears.

2. Click the New Message button on the Microsoft Exchange toolbar. The New Message dialog box appears (see Figure B.4).

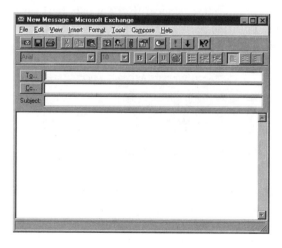

FIGURE B.4    The New Message dialog box.

3. Type your message. Then click the Send button on the New Message toolbar.

You can create customized views of the information stored in folders in Microsoft Exchange for easier retrieval and use.

To customize Microsoft Exchange:

1. Double-click the Inbox icon on the desktop. The Inbox Microsoft Exchange window appears.

2. Choose View, Columns on the Microsoft Exchange toolbar. The Columns dialog box appears (see Figure B.5).

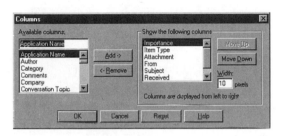

**FIGURE B.5** The Columns dialog box.

3. To add columns, select the columns in the Available Columns list you want to display on the right side of the Microsoft Exchange window. Then click the Add button.

4. To remove columns, select the columns in the Show the Following Columns list you don't want to display. Then click the Remove button.

5. To change the order of the columns, click the Move Up and Move Down buttons.

6. Choose OK to accept the changes you made to the columns in the Microsoft Exchange window.

7. To sort a column in the Microsoft Exchange window, choose View, Sort on the Microsoft Exchange menu bar. The Sort dialog box appears.

8. Choose the column you want to sort in the Sort Items By drop-down list. Choose the Ascending or Descending order option. Then choose OK to sort the column.

# INDEX